D0623786

PORTRAIT OF CAMUS

PORTRAIT OF CAMUS

An Illustrated Biography

Morvan Lebesque

Translated by T. C. Sharman

HERDER AND HERDER

1971
HERDER AND HERDER NEW YORK
232 Madison Avenue, New York 10016

Original edition: *Camus par lui-même,*
© 1963 by Éditions du Seuil, Paris.

Library of Congress Catalog Card Number: 70-167863
English translation © 1971 by Herder and Herder, Inc.
Manufactured in the United States

CONTENTS

On Monday the 4th of January 1960, at five minutes to two in the afternoon, on the road from Sens to Paris at a place called Villeblevin, a Facel-Vega sped past a peasant on a motorcycle. He heard a terrible noise and looked up to see, about a hundred yards ahead of him, that same car swerve, hit a tree, and then smash into another tree. In the field beside the car two women and the driver, Michel Gallimard, lay unconscious. A fourth passenger remained in the wreckage, already dead. An unused railway ticket was found in his pocket—he had decided to return from Lourmarin to Paris by car instead—and an identification card: Albert Camus, writer, born November 7, 1913, in Mondovi, Department of Constantine, Algeria.

A quiet funeral was held in the village where the accident had occurred, and he was buried in Lourmarin.

The entire world mourned his death, an untimely, unjust, most absurd death.

Algiers.

SUN AND HISTORY

IN 1961 Algeria became an independent state. In 1913, the year Camus was born, if anyone had predicted such an event, people would have laughed in his face. At that time, Algeria was quiet and seemed to have no problems; no one even thought of the possibility of that "unending little war on the fringe of the big wars" which a wise historian of the Second Empire foretold for France for the following century. It was half province, half colony, and two peoples lived side by side, the conqueror and the conquered, no one questioned the situation, at least the conqueror did not, and he was the only one who counted. And, if the word "racism" now finds its way into our text, let us not minimize it. There is much more to it than French contempt for the native or the anti-semitic disturbances in Algiers at the beginning of the century. What other word is there besides "racism" for the social discrimination which had then spread even into metropolitan France? Read the memoirs of the time (say Guéhenno's), find in their yellowing pages the pot-bellied bourgeois and the bony proletarian; consider the lady patrons who settle the social conflict with an alibi of charity while, from the time of Cavaignac, a strike-breaking army stands with arms at the ready, regarding the workers of Paris as no better than fellaheen. It's a faded picture, of course, for World War I, that mad adventure launched by the bourgeoisie

The Belle Époque in Algeria.

against its own self, brought these absurd values into collision. But we find them reflected in the Algeria of our own day, with the same unconcerned privileged class ("digestive tracts," President Sarraut called them), the same soldiers in the service of the "haves," the same distribution of food and clothing to the "have-nots" for the submissive gratitude which made Camus so indignant. There was a difference in Algeria: the lower classes had an extra stamp of inferiority, their sun-tanned hue, and any revolt could not be taken seriously, not even by their brethren, the lower-class Europeans, those firm supporters of colonial capitalism.

In 1913, Algeria was having its own belle époque; the "little fellow" in Europe might sometimes hoist and wave his red flag, but the "little fellow" in Algeria was quiet. It was the blessed hour of the fools who leave tragedy to their heirs. How could the French in Algeria have foreseen what was coming? With the good, quiet conscience of the Republic solidly behind them, what reason had they for winding their clocks and setting the alarm? They were safe in their right of possession and saw no need to say or do anything for it or even for themselves, for that matter—no more than a growing plant does. They would have been quite surprised to hear that one day one of them, a man of letters, would deliver an "Algerian message" to the world. A "message," what for? Their only thought was for *being,* for living, working, and getting on. For their minds, a bit of folklore was enough and they took it as simply as you sip a cocktail. At most, they waited for something without much caring, like a man in a hammock under the hot sun. "Gogol's Klestakov is met in Oran. He yawns and then: 'I feel I shall soon have to be concerned with something lofty.'"

And yet, the picture isn't true, it doesn't show the harsh reality of what the ordinary people saw. It is a man called Camus who will show us what Algeria was in 1913, not the Albert Camus we know but Lucien, his father.

Little is know of Lucien Camus, and that is a good thing; we can tell of his life in a few words, but they will be words of flesh and blood. Lucien led an exemplary life in his humble station, and it was a life, in fact, that was no more Algerian than the life he might have had in Brittany or in Picardy, for, leaving aside the sun and its glitter (though important enough, as we shall hear from his son), Lucien Camus' life of poverty was no different from what you could find in any corner of Metropolitan France. He was born poor and knew he would remain so. He was a farm laborer and obedient to his bosses. When he married, he took a woman of his own level; she was a servant of Spanish origin called Catherine Sintès and sister to all the Gomez and Hernandez tribe whom hunger in Spain had driven over to Africa. They had time for her to give him two sons. When the younger was hardly a year old, his father went off to France to get killed, in his zouave

11

Lucien Camus.

uniform. "At the battle of the Marne, his head split open. Blind and dying for a week: his name on the village war memorial."

And now it can all begin. The dead man was buried with so many others, far far from his native Africa, in the military cemetery at Saint-Brieuc where forty-three years later a new Nobel Prize winner was to come to pay his respects. The hospital sent the widow "a small shell splinter found in his body." Madame Camus, pressed no doubt by relations of hers, moved from Mondovi to Algiers. All she had was her pension and her strong arms; she took to "charring," and for the shelter of her brood

12

she quite naturally took a tiny apartment in the popular quarter of Belcourt.

Belcourt and Bab-el-Oued . . . To get back to them takes an effort. And yet it is not so distant a past, with men Camus knew and loved. Let us look at Belcourt with the eyes of the child Camus. It was a peaceable and cheerful working-class place, full of activity and color, intoxicated with itself. At Belcourt you were better than Algerian, you were Algiers, and you had no particular tenderness for the "barbarians" in other towns and none of course for the "Frenchies"; you followed strict customs and laws, not all of them written ones; you spoke the local dialect and embellished it with surprising turns: "Cocks' death! if I lie, let my skin peel off and my fice [face] come off . . ." There's a lot in it to remind us of the Marseilles of Maurice Pagnol, garlic, sunshine, gabble, it's another Marseilles raised to the tenth power.

When, however, you get to know Belcourt better, you find a deeper humanity under the folklore tatters, and a little later the young Camus did it justice in lines that we cannot read without emotion, lines that bring out a world now swept away. "At Belcourt, as at Bab-el-Oued, people get married young. They go to work early and in ten years exhaust the experience of a lifetime. A thirty-year-old workman has already played all the cards in his hand. He awaits the end between his wife and his children. His joys have been sudden and merciless, as has been his life. One realizes that he is born of this country where everything is given to be taken away . . . The notion of hell, for instance, is merely a funny joke here . . . Not that these men lack principles. They have their code and a very special one. You are not disrespectful to your mother. You see that your wife is respected in the street. You show consideration for a pregnant woman. You don't double up on an adversary, because 'that looks bad.' Whoever does not observe these elementary command-

13

The uncle's cooperage workshop, 1920.

ments, 'is not a man,' and the question is decided . . . But
at the same time the shopkeeper's ethics are unknown. I
have always seen faces around me filled with pity at the
sight of a man between two policemen. And before
knowing whether the man had stolen, killed his father, or
was merely a nonconformist, they would say: 'the poor
fellow' or else, with a hint of admiration: 'he's a pirate, all
right.'"

In these wonder-filled streets which sooner or later
were to disappear, war or no war, with history bowing to
"shopkeeper ethics" under this label and that, young
Albert whom his father had just had time to see before he
died, grew up between his mother's place and the workshop of an uncle who was a cooper by trade. "I think of a
child living in a poor district. That district, that house!
There were only two floors and the staircases were unlit
. . . On summer evenings, the working men go out on
to the balcony. In his flat, there was only one tiny window.
So they brought down the chairs and put them in front of

the house, and enjoyed the evening air . . . Summer evenings, mysteries with crackling stars! Behind the child lay a stinking corridor and his little chair, splitting across the bottom, sank slightly under his weight. But he had only to raise his eyes to drink straight from the pure sky.''

In 1919, this same child, in sailor-suit and sandals, entered primary school at Belcourt, to stay there until 1924, the final-certificate year when boys of his level in society had to give up schoolbooks for grownup tools. By good luck there was someone to stand against that usual fate: his teacher, M. Louis Germain, struck by the gifts he showed, put him in for the examination for scholarships to secondary school.

We doubt whether things went as simply as that. At that time the lower strata in Algiers had a strong prejudice against education. You were poor and you had to work with your hands, and the descendants of the pioneers were mistrustful of intellectuals. A friend of Camus told me he had to learn everything in secret with the fearful complicity of his family because a terrifying great-uncle, the head of the clan, threatened to shoot anyone who should think of putting Latin into the boy's head. Madame Camus couldn't read and we wonder how she took the teacher's idea. The important thing is that she said yes.

The secondary schools around 1925 were rather different from those of today. The middle classes held them to be the preserve of their sons, and the scholarship-boy from the proletariat was a bit like a boy receiving public assistance. He was supposed to work harder and be more serious than his fellows, for people were paying for him. Each day, the pupil Camus went from one world to another, from Belcourt to school, from the poor quarter to the rich boys' school, from the harsh life of the artisan to a soaring Valhalla of knowledge. He tells of the silence he met when he returned home, the curious indifference he noticed in his mother; it fascinated him and he was soon to discover it in himself. Silence and solitude . . . "The

15

child's mother never spoke either. Sometimes, people would ask her: 'What are you thinking about?' And she would reply: 'Nothing.' And that was the truth. Everything was already there, so she thought about nothing. Her life, her interests, her children were simply there, with a presence too natural to be felt . . . She is thinking of nothing. Outside, the light, the noises; here, silence in the night. The child will grow, will learn. They are bringing him up and will ask him to be grateful, as if they were sparing him pain. His mother will always have these silences. He will grow in pain. Being a man is what counts.''

It was a strange and fearful confrontation. Mother and son face to face, the boy finding his way by study and meditation into the great explanation of things, and his mother, quiet, deep, unseizable, and silent as the sea (Camus from an early stage linked the two words *mer* and *mere*), living, with an eternity of poverty and acquiescence

Goalkeeper (front row) for the Algiers University Racing Club.

behind her, in close intimacy with things. On the one side rebellion, and on the other the raw material for that rebellion and for going beyond it. But, here again, let us guard against a too facile interpretation. As the 30's opened, Camus' passion for justice was already stirring within him—social justice and simply Justice with a capital "J"—and he was preparing to fight, but what was boiling up in him did no harm either to his work or to his *joie de vivre*. Camus is not an impetuous and aggressive revolutionary. When we see him at the end of his schooldays, he is above all a youth glad to be alive, a handsome, dark young fellow with good muscles, a sportsman, and of marked Spanish type (and morally too! with the Castilian turn of mind which was to amuse his greatest master). This serious graduate was going on to a higher course in letters at the university. He was interested in amateur theatricals and football, and on Sundays he was at the goal line for the University Racing Club in a sky-blue and white sweater. It was on one of these Sundays that the first drama took place. In the evening, bathed in sweat after a hard match, Camus caught a chill and had to take to his bed. It was a lesion in the lung and then tuberculosis.

What are we to say of the part played by sickness in the personal make-up and the work of Camus? He himself, in the text with his clearest confidences in this connection (preface to *Betwixt and Between*), comments as follows: "That illness certainly added more fetters, and these were the hardest to bear, to those I already had. In the last resort it encouraged that freedom of the heart, that slight detachment from human concerns, which has always saved me from resentment . . . I have enjoyed it without restrictions or remorse." It probably served him, however, in another way, in strengthening his methodology. Few have been more methodical than Camus, few more obedient to their own rules, and there is no sacrilege in believing that he largely owed this discipline to the need not only of proving himself before death, which he had glimpsed so young (and which was to mock him so cruel- ly), should come, but also to the need of bending from a very early age to whatever unrevealed restrictions a sick person has to live with. At all events his illness had another consequence which is not in doubt, for it blocked the way to the career which Camus had mapped out for himself. Twice, in order to take an examination for his degree in philosophy, he had to face a medical test, and twice he was disqualified. This swept him off the path to what almost certainly otherwise lay in wait for him, being bogged down in teaching in Metropolitan France. At an age when not only a writer's vocation but also the themes and subjects of all his work are taking shape, Camus found himself forced first to stay on in Algeria, his homeland, and then, to earn a living, to take on a job which, paradoxically, was more dangerous for his health than teaching but so much more rewarding—journalism.

Would he have been "bogged down" all the same, or, to put it more clearly, did we almost have the literary generation of around 1945, Sartre, Camus and Simone de Beauvoir, enthroned as a trinity of philosophy professors? We may well believe it. It is true that in 1937 Camus refused a post offered him in the lycée of Sidi-bel-Abbès, but that was 1937, with a lot of other things behind him. In 1933, the young student in Algiers was still dreaming of Paris and the rue d'Ulm.* He was working for that and believed in it. At about this time, M. Jacques Heurgon tells us, "certain professors of the Faculty of Letters realized that a student of very rare quality was now among them." By "certain professors" you are to understand Jean Grenier. What Camus owed to Grenier he has shown and articulated clearly and often enough, not only in his writings but in a friendship which ended only with his death. He was working for a higher diploma on Plo-

*The street in Paris on which stands one of the highest institutes of learning for letters and philosophy.

tinus and St. Augustine, and he was reading Epictetus, Kierkegaard, Malraux, Gide, Proust, and Dostoevsky. He contracted around this time two engagements which came to a rapid end. The first was a hasty marriage such as a young man can enter into when he is sensual and an idealist at one and the same time; the marriage broke up in 1934. The second was joining the Communist Party; two years later his membership card had been torn up. Laval had been to Moscow to get Stalin to tell the French Communists to change their policy of support for Moslem claims. The militant Camus was automatically ordered to change his attitude. He refused and was expelled from the Party.

We see him now married and divorced by 20, with illness barring the road to the university, and again out of the political church where he thought to find a family. On top of all this, he managed to lose the small clerk's job which someone had gotten him in the Prefecture; the reason given was that he would not stick to the "pure administrative style" in writing his reports. What was he to do now? Nothing but wait and suffer poverty and loneliness. From this moment his was the existence of the bastard writer, the product of his time and its bad organization. The State had given the school boy Camus just enough to make him one of its highly educated servants. The sickly graduate of the seminary of the world now fell below the level of the proletariat, a broken promise, a man without job or future. Emmanuel Roblès, who knew him already, spoke soberly of "these hard years." Camus, in very truth, knew the depths of poverty. He was living on boulevard Saint-Saëns, in the middle of the city, "in a bare room with only a long chest to sleep on and keep his things in. His books were stacked on the floor and against the walls." I like to think that this was the room where Pascal Pia came to find him one day to propose the launching of a newspaper, the *Alger Républicain.*

19

The new paper was to be "different"; it seemed to be the right time for it. Algeria, like France, was stirring. The Popular Front Government, like a wedge driven into history, had cut French political life into two eras. Before it, the bourgeois system based on artificial prosperity and bankrupted by the terrible slump of the 30's; and now, social legislation and a mad pursuit of justice and a better life for all. In Algeria, however, the decisive step was not to be taken and the Blum-Violette project was stifled. The French settlers in Algeria vowed: "Not even in the smallest place shall we ever allow an Arab to become a mayor."

Alger Républicain, a quarter of a century ahead of the ideas of a famous general and President of the Republic, believed the Algeria of that time was doomed beyond recourse; you could not eternally keep a people under tutelage on its own soil. The immense wealth on one side would sooner or later be defeated by the immense poverty on the other. The wages of an Arab, for equal work, must be equal to a European's. The Arab child had a right to schooling and its parents to the benefits of the new social legislation. These were the convictions of Pascal Pia; he was a strange, likeable, Roman-nosed giant, an expounder of Guillaume Apollinaire, who, in his leisure hours, enjoyed hoaxing the literary men. Camus without hesitation adopted the views of Pia and accepted the reporter's job that was offered him.

From the outset Camus' journalistic career with *Alger Républicain* was difficult, dangerous in every respect, and scandal-raising. The paper, in direct rivalry with the powerful *Echo d'Alger,* which was soon to be the paper of the ultra-reactionaries, was badly-off and threatened on all sides. To keep down his expenses, Camus at the risk of his health went about the hard way, would avoid hotels and get a bed with sympathizers. His articles were immediately in violent contrast with what the compliant Algerian press was printing. To mention only three of them: the *Hodent*

20

affair, in which he proved that a poor farm laborer was innocent of the theft he was accused of by a rich settler; the *El-Okby affair,* in which he demonstrated the innocence of the Mohammedan who was accused of murder by order of the authorities for purely political reasons; and the *La Martinière affair* where he rose in protest against the inhuman conditions in which convicts were shipped to Guiana. "It is not pity that is called for but something quite different. There is nothing more abject to be seen than men degraded below the condition of man." Here we have already a glimpse of the "great Camus" and we are shortly to see, in the celebrated *Kabylia Inquiry* the addition of a kind of icy and painful humor—note for instance how he lists all the excellent reasons trotted out by the settler for perpetuating the miserable poverty of the Moslems and for putting a stamp of nobility on it into the bargain. When we re-read these articles, we cannot help admiring their weight and balance, for they have nothing to say which is not reasonable. There is one dominating theme almost everywhere: the Arab uprooted in his own country.

In the matter of style, Camus did not give himself the trouble of developing anything special and made no difference between writing for the press and his style in more serious work; his prose had a natural nobility and lost nothing in scorning "punch" and journalistic sensationalism. Meantime, however, the reporting job did teach him the value of concrete statement and a dislike of obscure formulas. Camus wrote to be understood and avoided all unclarity and all base desire to please. And, we may be sure, he was understood only too well. By 1938 indignant voices were heard attacking this journalist who was not playing the game; he was already being treated as an undesirable and people were predicting that sooner or later "something would happen to him."

How magnificently carefree youth can be! Not only did Camus have no fear of "something happening" but his work as a journalist was not enough for him. His leaning towards the theater reasserted itself and he devoted his leisure time to organizing a troupe of amateur players. The new company, "The Team," found its inspiration in the principles of Copeau. There was little scenery; the actor and the text were everything. Camus, in very truth, had his finger in every pie. He was author, actor, producer, effects man, and prompter. Performances were given in the open air or in little suburban halls. The repertory was wide and covered *La Celestine* by Rojas, *Le Paquebot Tenacity* by Vildra, *L'Article 330* by Courteline, *The Playboy of the Western World* by Synge, Gide's *Retour de L'Enfant Prodigue* (in which Camus devised, for the younger son's final flight to life and freedom, a gateway "very high and very narrow"), and lastly *Brothers Karamazov*, in which he took the part of Ivan. *Brothers Karamazov* was one of the highlights of the undertaking, and Camus had already in mind to adapt *The Possessed.* Meanwhile he had written *Revolt in Asturia,* his first published work, and produced it in a style of popular dramatic experiment. He could no longer doubt his many-sided vocation as a writer, any more than he could doubt the Algerian landscape from which it took its soaring flight.

In those early years, hard, perilous, impatient times, everything was possible, not only the installation of a free interracial community which would make Algeria, at the crossroads of two continents, a bi-racial country in which two rooted peoples lived together in exemplary fraternity, but also the beginnings of a personality of universal dimension. The French in Algeria are greater than they think, only their greatness is a rather different one from the one they think of. This is a small nation lacking traditions but not lacking poetry, and there were a number of writers, including Jean Grenier, Claude de Freminville (a printer as well as a writer), Réné-Jean Clot (a painter as well as a writer), and first and foremost Gabriel Audisio,

the author of *Jeunesse de la Mediteranée* and *Sel de la Mer,*
who had understood that the nation had something to say
or, in an expression which is displeasing but commonly
used, it had a message. A hundred years had gone by since
the conquest, and it could be thought that the time had
come to decipher the message, to make a civilization out
of a military hazard of history and give precedence to the
pioneers of the spirit over the pioneers of the soil. The
undertaking was of course still ill-defined (and ten years
later, when the School of Algiers had conquered Paris, it
was to be seen that like all the other schools—and what is
more natural?—it served only to publicize one or two
second-class writers, while the others were well able to
impose thenselves by their own efforts). Its stock-in-trade
was a few words: *youth, sea,* and *sun,* which intoxicated its
members in the extreme. And yet you can feel that the
words here have a full and deep meaning—would they one
day succeed in giving them body? *Youth, sea,* and *sun*—
after all they are words which rang out in Greece thousands of years ago at the starting point of one of the
greatest adventures mankind has seen. It was an adventure
which the leaders of the School of Algiers believed in with
all their might, and in their ambition to live it again they
had already found the essential thing, a Maecenas. This
was Charlot, a bookseller, who turned publisher and
turned out masses of tracts, booklets, and manifests, as
well as a review under the title *Rivages.* Anyone who was a
seeker, anyone who foresaw that "something is going to
happen" and madly desired to be there when it did,
anyone who deeply felt the lyricism of the Mediterranean
without being able, alas, to find the master words to
express it, could be found at Charlot's. And one evening,
as was to be expected, someone brought Camus. It was an
historic evening: with the companions of Ulysses waiting,
Ulysses arrives in person. For Camus, we know, was not
seeking; he had found. In the course of his Odyssey, in the

23

The Algerian coastline.

hazards of a hard life, in his joys and angers, in the lines of his fate and in those of his native land, he had found the direction his thought and work were to take.

Youth, sea, and *sun* . . . and we must add *history* and *death.* Camus, at 25, is ready. "A liquid morning rose, dazzling, over the pure sea. From the sky, fresh as a rose, washed and rewashed by the waters, reduced by each successive laundering to its most delicate and clearest texture, there fell a quivering light which gave each house, each tree, a palpable shape and a magic newness. The earth, on the morning the world was born, must have arisen in just such a light.'' First and foremost, Camus' work tells of the shock which one and all meet in Algeria—dazzlement is the word.

You could believe yourself in a land blessed of the gods and it was a formula Camus himself fell for. "In spring, Tipasa is inhabited by gods and the gods speak in the sun and the scent of absinthe leaves . . .'' but only to take it back straightway: "Those who need myths here are indeed poor . . . And what need have I to speak of Dionysus to say that I love to crush mastic bowls under my nose''? For, in Algeria, there are no gods. Nature in Algeria seems to suffice unto herself, perhaps because the country lies between two unpeopled immensities, the Sahara and the sea. Did I say the gods were not there? It is rather that God is not there. For, no more than Camus was, shall we be taken in by the pious invocations in multi-colored beads left to rot in the cemeteries of Algiers; here there is only the joy of the hour, free of all metaphysics. In the city, as soon as the brief winter is over, men and women have only one thought, to dash to the beaches and sacrifice to the sun. "What you can love in Algiers is what everyone lives off: the sea visible at every corner . . .'' Algiers is the capital of the fleeting moment and, in that, so truly the gate of Africa, that immense continent where the more you advance the more you realize with stupor that the future here has no meaning, so little that the natives connot comprehend the missionary when he talks to them of a "life to come.'' "You doubtless need to spend a long time in Algiers to understand how dessicating an excess of nature's blessings can be. There is nothing here for people seeking knowledge, education, and self-improvement . . . Throughout their

25

"What meaning can such words as future, well-being, your place in the world have here?" Tipasa.

youth, men find here a life which matches their beauty. Then, afterwards, come decline and forgetfulness. They have wagered on the flesh, but they knew that they would lose. In Algiers . . . for the man who has lost his youth there is nothing to hang on to, and no place where melancholy can escape from itself."

The provisional, the fleeting moment, the hour of noon hanging in the sky: "What meaning can such words as future, well-being, your place in the world have here?" Surely one does better to give oneself up to the passing hour and plunge into it as another dives into the sea? "Vast sea, forever virgin and forever ploughed, my religion with the night!" And what is the sea? It is Proudhon who whispers the answer to Camus: it is freedom. Listen how Camus intones his hymn to the sea and to freedom, a canticle of joyous immersion: "I must be naked and dive into the sea, still scented with the perfumes of the earth, wash these off in the sea, and consummate on my flesh the embrace for which sun and sea, lips to lips, have so long been sighing. I feel the shock of the water, rise up through a thick, cold glue, then dive back with my ears ringing, my nose streaming, and the taste of salt in my mouth. As I swim, my water-varnished arms flash out to turn gold in the sunlight and then plunge back with a twist of all my muscles; the water streams along my whole body as my legs take tumultuous possession of the waves—and the horizon disappears. On the beach, I flop down on the sand, yield to the world, feel my flesh and bones heavy again, besotted with sunlight, occasionally glancing at my arms where the water slides off and patches of salt and soft blond hair appear on my skin."

It was at Tipasa that Camus sang. Tipasa is a ruined Roman city with, nowadays, fishermen's villages grafted onto it. Their pathways run along the ancient Roman streets. Ruined columns, the color of pine, take the place of eucalyptus trees. Tamarisk and absinthe bushes grow between abandoned stone coffins. Camus went there often, never to stay more than a day, for the early born need of moderation which Mediterranean wisdom had taught him bade him not to squander his pleasures. He never concealed what he came to seek in these surroundings, it was primarily joy, the sheer joy of living. For "there is no shame in being happy and I call fools those who fear pleasure." At the root of everything is sensuous pleasure. "How many hours spent crushing absinthe leaves, caressing ruins, trying to match my breathing to the tumultuous sighs of the world!" It was here that Camus understood for the first time that "his kingdom is entirely of this world" and that he "will never approach closely enough to it." "Here I understand what is called glory: the right to love without restraint. There is only one love in this world. Embracing a woman's body also means holding in your arms this strange joy which desends from sky to sea. In a moment, when I throw myself down among the absinthe plants to bring their scent into my body, I shall know, whatever prejudices may say, that I am fulfilling a truth which is that of the sun and which will also be that of my death. In a sense, it is indeed my life that I am playing out here, a life which tastes of warm stone, is full of the sighs of the sea and the rising song of the crickets. The breeze is cool and the sky blue. I love life with abandon and wish to speak of it with freedom: it makes me proud of my human condition. Yet people have often told me: there's nothing to be proud of. Yes, there is: this sun, this sea, my heart leaping with youth, the salt taste of my body, and the vast landscape where tenderness and glory merge in blue and yellow. It is this conquest that requires my strength and my resources. Everything here leaves me intact, I give up nothing of myself, I put on no mask: it is enough for me patiently to acquire the difficult knowledge of how to live which is worth all their arts of living."

"Joy and life" will be the verdict of the hasty reader. But let him take careful note of another chord which came so naturally to Camus' pen: *death* and *sun*.

Below a certain line of latitude where rain, wind, and

cold are halted, the sun speaks only of life—*Mehr Licht!*
And yet, the farther you advance southward the more you
meet death at every step, a fearsome and everyday thing.
It is only in northern latitudes that death has charms for
the poets, the sun, a maker of rotting corpses, shows us
death unveiled. More than any others, Camus felt the
truth of this and knew that light "in its compactness
freezes the world and the things in it in a dark dazzlement." In 1937, with a cheap ticket, he went to Florence,
and the cemeteries haunt the record we owe to that visit.
He was in Fiesole in the splendid height of summer and it
was a skull on a Franciscan table that captivated his eyes.
And could she be anywhere but in Algiers, that old woman
of *Betwixt and Between,* patiently waiting out her time by
her own funeral vault, the only luxury and the only reward
of her life?

It was the sun, as much as illness, that brought it home
to Camus that he was mortal. That he was doomed sooner
or later to that "disgusting and terrifying adventure"
against which he revolted with all his being: "I said no. I
said no with all the strength in me." It was a useless revolt,
for every life, as the tombstones tell us, is *"col sol levante,
col sol cadente."* "But even today, I fail to see how its
uselessness weakens my revolt and I have a clear feeling of
the strength it draws from it."

Sunrise and sunset . . . there is a day, it can be longer
or shorter, more or less filled, with its joys, its wonder-
ments, and its certainties—I know this world is truly my
kingdom and I am happy in it—and then comes night and
death, and tomorrow. For others, there is another awak-
ening and, for them too, night and death. But the sun
taught Camus another truth, a truth that was to magnify
his work and set him in full counter-stream to the writers
of his generation.

Of an evening, after an unhurried stroll along the shore
of Tipasa or a long walk on the neighboring hills ("I was

learning to breathe, I was completing and accomplishing myself"), Camus would find himself again in a public garden by the roadside. There, "as I left the tumult of scents and sunlight," watching "the countryside fill out with light," no doubt, despite the joy of having quite fulfilled his "task as a man," of having "played" his "part well," that is, of having, like an actor, entered "a ready-made pattern" and brought "it to life with" his "own heartbeats," no doubt he stood and sized up the astonishing contradictions of sea and sun. Life, and death afterwards, were a broken line only in appearance. In reality it was a continuity, a higher, fearsome, and un-decipherable continuity in which he merged entirely, embracing the universe, and a continuity from which one day he would be excluded and cast out. And then, there was another enigma. At Tipasa he could, true enough, "join in the festivals of earth and beauty," drink his fill of the sublimity of tragedy, feel with all his being that "accord of earth with man freed of his human element—ah! if I were not already a worshipper I should present myself as a convert!"—until he met the temptation even of giving up all other endeavors, including the ambition of artistic creation. "What do we accomplish? O bitter bed, princely couch, the crown lies at the bottom of the seas." But, despite everything, the day, he knew, was ended, and he must, quite simply, "go home," go back to the city, with "his bathing costume still damp and wound round his fist" as the friends he met would see him, back to the poor quarter, "back to the paraffin lamp and the oilcloth," and fit into circumscribed space and circumscribed time. "Ris-ing, tram, four hours in the office or the factory, meal, tram, four hours of work, meal, sleep and Monday, Tuesday, Wednesday, Thursday, Friday, and Saturday, according to the same rhythm." In a word, it was back to poverty.

Not that poverty worried him so much. Anyone close to

Camus knew how much he was detached from riches. As it is said, there are some people whose fingers riches do not stick to, and Camus was one of these. He himself spoke of this in unassuming tones. "I sometimes meet people who live in the midst of fortunes that I cannot even imagine. I still have to make an effort to realize that others can feel envious of these fortunes . . . I learned a truth that has always led me to greet the signs of comfort, or of a well-appointed house, with irony, impatience, or sometimes with fury. I do not know how to own things . . . I cling like a miser to that liberty which immediately disappears with the arrival of excessive wealth . . . I love the bare interior of houses in Spain or North Africa. The place where I prefer to live and work (and, something more rare, where I would not mind dying) is a hotel bedroom." But you have already understood that, if he hardly applied the word poverty to himself and his circumstances, he also did not fence it in with narrow meaning. Poverty and misery for him was a sign of the condition of man, the sign of all the struggles to be waged against blind illogical forces, against injustice and oppression. It was the sign of *facts*. In short, it was history.

History is not to be cheated. You, child of sea and sun, you who claim to be a cousin of the Greeks and invoke them, you are an Algerian born of a farm laborer father and a servant mother, and the first of your fellows you meet in the street will bring you back to the fold. For history exists, in the young workman with brilliantined hair or the old woman alone with her lamp, and history is as real and as great as elemental continuity. It is "men's desperate endeavor to give substance to the most prophetic of their dreams." Society has seen in it its supreme demand and made it its god, and a god how hard, implacable, and exclusive! "What are the sorrows of Iphigenia to me," asked Goethe, "when the weavers of Weimar are dying of hunger?" He wrote Iphigenia all the same, and

31

found time to polish it and finish it off—of course he had closed his window. But today the window would not close tightly, and the moans of the weavers would break into the high endeavor. You have to choose; at a certain level of efficiency, below which there is nothing serious, you cannot be poet and militant at one and the same time.

On the contrary, however, it was the genius of Camus to show that the choice had not to be made. In more precise terms, he reminded us—and how great was our need of it!—that there are two sides in man, the side of eternity and the side of history, each distinct and both requiring to be fulfilled under pain of mutilation, the mutilation inflicted on themselves by so many French writers between 1940 and 1960, some of them frozen in ''art for art's sake'' and the rest in mere efficiency, and this a poor thing anyhow. What led Camus to this conclusion was of course his following of the precept ''Know thyself.'' He had not taken long to sound the depth of riches in his poverty. A little astonished at first: ''I lived with very little money, but also in a kind of rapture . . .'' Then, analyzed: ''It was not poverty that stood in the way of my strength: in Africa, the sun and the sea cost nothing.'' Developed: ''Poverty, first of all, was never a misfortune for me: it was radiant with sunlight . . .'' Concluded: ''An extreme state of poverty has always something in common with the luxury and the riches of the world . . . Poverty has its • loneliness, but it is a loneliness which helps to put the right value on everything we meet.''

From that point it was only a step to being resigned and being one of ''the enlightened poor'' contented with their lot and deciding that, since the rest of the poor were in the same boat, everything was for the best in the best of worlds. But Camus was too clear-thinking to fall into that ''shopkeeper's morality.'' There was solid evidence before his eyes. ''Happiness requires a certain frame of mind but poverty will sooner prepare you for a silent, lonely

32

death than induce that frame of mind." And more: "With fifteen thousand francs a month coming in and a job in the workshop, Tristan finds nothing to talk to Isolde about." It was no time for singing, with Gentleman Faust on the air of sweet-singing Gounod: "What riches I find in this poverty!" For Tristan to have something to say—a matter of capital importance, for this is love and the whole world is at stake—he must have the conditions for it, that is, history must be made. "You can't get away from it," you are in it "up to the neck." But even in history, "you may insist on fighting to preserve the part of man that does not belong to him." For "there is history and there is the rest, simple happiness, enthusiasm for living things, natural beauty," all "roots that history knows not," but requiring you to fight for them as you fight the fight of history. There is a double victory to be won; otherwise, there is only defeat on both fields.

"Even my revolts were lit up by the sun. These revolts were almost always, I think I can say this in all honesty, revolts on everyone's behalf, aimed at lifting up everybody's life into the light. Quite possibly my heart was not naturally disposed to this kind of love. But circumstances helped me. To correct my natural indifference, I was placed half-way between poverty and the sun. Poverty prevented me from thinking that all is well under the sun and in history; the sun taught me that history is not everything. Change life, yes, but not the world which I worshipped as a God. It is thus, no doubt, that I embarked upon my present difficult career, stepping innocently onto a tightrope along which I now move painfully forward, unsure of ever reaching the end. In other words, I became an artist, if it is true to say that there is no art without refusal or consent."

Nearly twenty years after these meditations at Tipasa, Camus came back to roam throughout the ruined city. A war had swept through the world and Tipasa bore the absurd marks it had left, barbed wire, "No entry after closing time," a custodian in uniform. The changes Camus found were for him the symbol of the page of history which the peoples of the world had just turned, of the bloody revolution which the wheel of time had just completed. He had been part of all that and now he was here again, with the stones, the coffins, the shore and the sea, a man loyal to a dual truth he had been taught in this very place. History and the sun, he had seen to it that each had its share. "I have denied nothing of the country of my birth and at the same time I have not closed my eyes to any of the servitudes of the times I live in." Loyally and with a clear head he had followed the path traced before him; loyally and with a clear head he had devoted himself to the two influences, "even when, particularly when, they seemed contradictory." He had followed, there and back, the road that leads from "the uplands of the spirit to the high places of crime." He had remained faithful to a dual memory, that of "beauty and the humiliated." And he was more and more persuaded that "to refuse a part of what is, is to refuse to be, oneself. It is like letting someone else do your living for you."

A dual truth, a dual influence, a dual memory. It was all the harmony of the life of man that the young Albert Camus had culled from the lesson of sun and sea. Now he was approaching the threshold of his career, an "artist," if you like, but first of all a universal man, living at once in his mortal times and in all others; a man able to express what is eternal and to make history from day to day; possessing the great wisdom taught to the Greeks by the sun, which tells us that what is called progress is not a rising straight line but movement in a circle and inexhaustible. Harmony . . . yes, harmony. Only, in the so much admired machine you could hear the grain of sand grinding; it was a small thing set on one side at the beginning of all meditation and, perhaps, forgotten by the reader:

34

There is no God, or rather, God is unimaginable and is not even to be imagined. God absent, even the desire of God absent. And since the world is without reason or end, without design, since no will informs it, since eternity is void, you may meditate, you may act and do, but no vain noises you call forth will stop your ears or hide from you the grinding of the grain of and in the machine. Until you acknowledge it. And admit it. And give it its name.

This grain of sand, no, not a grain of sand, it is the motive force itself—it has its name in fact, it is called the Absurd.

THE ABSURD

The 2nd of September 1939 was to be a red-letter day. It was the day Camus was to go on vacation with his fiancée and future second wife, Francine Faure. They were off to Greece, his land of desire, on a journey so long dreamt of. All this at least was what the steamer ticket promised, bought several days in advance and religiously tucked away in his wallet.

On the 2nd of September 1939 there was no dreamy departure for Greece, only a call to join the newspaper team summoned to hurry to the Government General and receive the new instructions of wartime censorship. Camus complied, grumbling—it was no affair of his, he was going to enlist. He was reckoning without his state of health which, once more, disqualified him.

War has sometimes its good side. For instance, it enables the Authorities to tame certain rebellious spirits and take revenge for their peacetime attitudes. It was now clear from the first day that *Alger Républicain* was going to pay dearly for its liberal views. You could say they were

Kabylia.

out of luck. Only a month or two before the "new turn of events" the paper had published, over the signature of A. Camus, the famous *Kabylia Inquiry* denouncing backwardness, want, and famine in a whole province. "Very early one morning at Tizi-Ouzou I saw children in rags fighting with dogs over what was in a dustbin . . ." Such lines are unforgettable, and so are these: "When I asked a Kabyle, he told me: 'It's like that every morning.' In the Djemaa-Saridj area, the men (Arabs) get 8 to 10 francs a day, and the women five. Around Michelet, the average farm worker gets 5 francs, with food, for a ten-hour day. But arrears of taxes are deducted without telling the wage earner and sometimes the deductions amount to as much as all the wage. Nine hundred thousand native children at present are getting no schooling . . ."

Obviously, such a report filled with facts and figures, sounded a discordant note in higher spheres of an Administration accustomed to the lazy purring of the official press ("the Kabyle peasant, so fatalistic and picturesque"), and so did Camus' conclusion in which he rejected the palliative of charity (a few pounds of wheat

36

for a whole village donated by a "charitable soul"), demanded justice, and—the sacrilege of it!—did not shrink from citing the example of a Kabyle village which had obtained permission to look after its own affairs and had succeeded where the Government General had failed miserably. Not to speak of the report's frankly intolerable tone: "It is contemptible to say that the Kabyle people adapt themselves to poverty and want. It is contemptible to say that these people have not the same needs as we have . . . It is curious to see how a people's qualitites can be used to justify the state of degradation in which it is held and see the Kabyle peasant's proverbial frugality called upon to justify the hunger that gnaws at his vitals."

From the same 2nd of September, two military censors, "two cavalry captains full of disdain and with no attempt to conceal their distaste" (Emm. Roblès), took up permanent quarters in the newspaper's offices. The only way to cope with the presence of the two scissor-wielding bullies was with humor (and of this I shall speak in a later chapter). However, as you might expect, humor won a battle or two but lost the war. Eventually the Government General made the "unavoidable decision" to advise Albert Camus, aged 26, profession: journalist, to leave Algiers. The advice sounded rather like expulsion.

Once more, what was to be done? His friend Pia advised Camus to cross the sea and sent him to *Paris-Soir,* where he was accepted as editorial secretary. It was the spring of 1940 and the middle of the "phoney war." Camus never told me about the short period of his life when he discovered Paris, a capital still under suspended sentence where people were seriously beginning to believe that everything would end without bloodshed. "The iron road is cut." "We shall win, we shall win because we are stronger." One morning, Paris woke with a start and rushed madly onto the roads, and unending lines of ordinary Frenchmen, marching on dumbfounded were mas-

37

Camus with Pascal Pia, 1940.

sacred by swastika aircraft on the bridges over the Loire River. The elegant war correspondents of vague rank in their spanking uniforms had suddenly given up bolstering civilian morale. Newspapers fell back and *Paris-Soir* found a refuge in Clermont-Ferrand, taking Camus along. He had hardly had time to get to know Paris and had started his wanderings again, with a minimum of luggage, but in a bag he had with him he carried the manuscript of *The Stranger* which he had finished on the 8th of May, thirty-six hours before the battle broke.

In June 1940, Hitler paraded down the Champs-Elysées, and in July the "armistice line" cut France in two. The French were beaten and there were Frenchmen who hurried to let them know it. As predictably as the progression of a virus infection, defeat brings political reaction. Camus again met the men of the Algiers censorship, with other faces but the same uniforms, the only difference being that now they were more powerful than ever, a conquering defeated gang. He left *Paris-Soir* and found a refuge in Lyons, and at the end of 1940 he married again.

I suppose I have no need to stress—but perhaps so, nonetheless, for so many confuse the French people with the various regimes they saw come and go—that Camus was never the enemy of a country but only of political regimes. Between 1937 and 1939, in *Alger Républicain,* he had spoken out against Franco and in defense of the Spanish republicans (and, to the day of his death, in the atmosphere of weak acceptance of the Iberian dictator into which France gradually slipped, he was among the last of the unreconciled). In 1939, he never spoke of "war against Germany" but only of "war against Hitler." By 1940, his celebrated *Letters to a German Friend* awaited only their final shape. In the midst of the noise and tumult of Hitleran "grandeur," Camus was well aware that "justice is the only greatness of a country." With Europe under the conqueror's heel, he looked the conqueror in the face. "You know what the conqueror is looking for right and left? It is not unity, which is above everything the harmony of contrasts; it is totality, the crushing out of differences." The "new Europe" patched up by the Nazis and the cheap-Jack "new France" it included could only be for him a prison and in it he roamed back and forth, looking for a way out everywhere, first of all in himself. The prison was not so big; after three months in Lyons, Camus returned to Algeria, not to Algiers but to Oran, where his wife's family took him in.

Oran, the second city in Algeria and worthy to be the capital of the country, Oran which "has its back to the sea," though built on one of the finest bays in the world, received with magnificent indifference this "limpid and ravaged" traveler who had been to France and back with nothing to show for it. The same tale goes on, no job, hardly any money; moreover, he had on his shoulders the weight of an irony that well deserves another name. *Absurdity* it certainly was, but which of them was *absurd*, the world or Camus? He, at all events, found in solitude the energy to finish off his first works. He was no longer quite a beginner in the world of letters. In Algiers, Charlot had already brought out for him two slim volumes, *Betwixt and Between* and *Nuptials. The Stranger,* a mere outcrop in a rich subsoil, was now completed. *Caligula* had been begun as far back as 1938, *Cross Purpose* was in gestation, and the first pages of *The Myth of Sisyphus* had flashed into being. The extremities of the cycle of the absurd had met and closed.

We come to *The Stranger.* But first of all, we will scrape the canvas or, better, X-ray it to get at the original picture.

His first name was Patrice Meursault. And he was not alone, for by his side he had an admirable mentor, the manly and wise friend Zagreus, who one day realized that only an act from which there could be no returning would save the young man from the elemental evil of all-devouring time and a life without meaning. Therefore Zagreus patiently armed the spirit of Patrice and strengthened his arm; he allowed him to murder him, freeing him of blame in advance by means of a letter which was his testament. Through this ritual and even magic murder (since for Zagreus you must read Dionysos), Patrice finally reaches the "presence," that is, through the byways of social power, he attains the highest liberty which is mastery over time. Hence the title of the novel (as written in 1937): *The Happy Death,* linking back to the poet's joyous immersion in the sea. This was a legend novel which three years ripening transformed into a tale of high perfection, freed of all temptations to symbolism, so that, when it appeared, some saw only its fire, and not the fire of the

Orphic sacrifice, but the flickering oil lamp of the novels ''of the people'' in the fashion of 1930.

Since, after all, that takes nobody in and everyone knows *The Stranger,* let us divert ourselves with a profile:

''Young Meursault has a small clerking job in an Algiers office; he is lonely and poor. When the novel opens, he has been informed that his mother has died in an old people's home. He asks his employer for two days off for the funeral. When he comes back, he takes up his old habits and neighbors, Céleste, Masson, old Salamano, and Marie Cardano, a typist who some time back had worked with him in the same place and whom he 'had desired at the time.' A love affair springs up between boy and girl, and Marie becomes Meursault's mistress. Some time after this, Meursault gets to know a certain Raymond Sintès, who becomes his friend and takes him off to the beach. There is a quarrel with an Arab, and a row. Raymond lends his revolver to Meursault who kills the Arab.'' But we must stop; this is a game and not a game, for it is not so sure that Camus' style has not borrowed from that pedestrian literature. It is a strange style with a mixing of sentences so dissimilar as ''I had a busy morning in the office. My employer was in a good humor. He even inquired if I wasn't too tired'' and ''gazing up at the dark sky spangled with its signs and stars, for the first time, the first, I laid my heart open to the benign indifference of the universe.'' Here also in fact the ''dual truth'' reigns and imposes a dual tone, the tone of the fleeting instant and that of eternity, want and the sun, history and tragedy.

History is the life of Meursault as he tells it. Tragedy is the fate which, unknown to him, the world and the sun are preparing for him. Max Jacob, before his martyr's death, had the time to read *The Stranger* and defined it as a ''study of a man insensitive to present reality.'' Insensitive? We would rather say absent, absent like the ordainer of har-

41

mony at Tipasa who was not to be found. Once more there bursts into the world of letters a challenge to God, thrown down not by Faust nor by Don Juan, but by a mere little clerk in Algiers, and what we hear is not a cry of revolt nor the utterance of a threat, but an echo.

"God not here," says Nature. "Me not here," is Meursault's reply. And he thinks, speaks, and acts as if indeed he were not there. Absent-present at his mother's funeral, absent-present at the cinema where the very next day he takes Marie to see a Fernandel film, absent-present in bathing on the beach, in events at home and in the street, in the friendships and love that are offered him. "It's all the same" is his key expression. Two or three times, when a question he cannot evade is put, he calmly replies "No." "Marie came that evening and asked me if I'd marry her. I said I didn't mind; if she was keen on it, we'd get married.

"Then she asked me again if I loved her. I replied, much as before, that her question meant nothing or next to nothing—but I supposed I didn't.

"'If that's how you feel, she said, 'why marry me?'

"I explained that it had no importance . . .

"Then she remarked that marriage was a serious matter.

"To which I answered: 'No.'"

The whole story is told in a first person which is paradoxically impersonal, and in a perfect tense which deadens the impact of the event, withdraws it and dims it (it is a tense so eminently anti-novel that, before *The Stranger* no one thought it possible to use it from beginning to end of a story). And yet it has nothing in common with the behaviorism of American novels of the same time which Camus so rightly detested, saying "I would give a hundred Hemingways for a Stendhal or a Benjamin Constant." No, what we have here is not duty-scamping literature recording only the reactions of robots, we have a deep and full confession in "an undramatizing voice," to

42

take the admirable words of M. Jean-Claude Brisville. "Mother died today. Or, maybe, yesterday; I can't be sure. The telegram from the Home says: 'Your mother passed away. Funeral tomorrow, Deep sympathy.' Which leaves the matter doubtful; it could have been yesterday."

But what about the actual deed, the crime? Well, here again, Meursault is simply not there. His pal, Raymond, a cheap-minded hooligan, has left him behind on the beach, with a revolver in his pocket. The quarrelsome Arab has gone to lie down on the sand in the shadow of a rock. Meursault crosses in front of him, with no bad intention. "My impression had been that the incident was closed." But there is the sun "like a blade of vivid light" flashing on "a sea of molten steel" and the blade of the knife the Arab has taken out as a measure of precaution. "A dazzling sheen of light" is crowding up behind Meursault, time is suspended, stopped, nailed to the zenith beside the flaming orb of the sun. It is the great tragic stillness of noon. Noon, and not midnight, is the hour of the deed. "Then everything began to reel before my eyes, a fiery gust came from the sea, while the sky cracked in two, from end to end, and a great sheet of flame poured down through the rift. Every nerve in my body was a steel spring, and my grip closed on the revolver. The trigger gave, and the smooth underbelly of the butt jogged my palm. And so, with that crisp whip-crack sound, it all began. I shook off my sweat and the clinging veil of light. I knew I'd shattered the balance of the day, the spacious calm of this beach on which I had been happy. But I fired four shots more into the inert body, on which they left no visible trace. And each successive shot was another loud, fearful rap on the door of my undoing."

The tale could have ended there, but then it would have been short of the other side, the reply of men, his "brothers," to Meursault and their ridiculous endeavors to fill in the emptiness of his life, doing "as if," as if God

43

existed, as if life had a meaning, answering the workings of fate with their little devices. So Meursault is apprehended by the judges. Everybody is a judge, policemen, magistrates, the lawyer himself, and even the public in the assize court. Why did he kill? First of all, who is he? This has got to be known, because they have to "understand." There will be punishment of course, but not before they have understood. Prisoner in the dock, explain yourself. You say you can't? Very well, we'll explain you ourselves. No need of more than a short trial with each act of the "criminal" examined under the magnifying glass all the same. The diagnosis reached is not hard to guess—an old mother buried without any tears, a Fernandel film for a funeral oration, the escapade with a typist the very next day, it all goes to show that what we have here is a monster, something very simple and very ordinary and easy to explain. What is he to answer? "I rose, and as I felt in the mood to speak, I said the first thing that crossed my mind: that I'd had no intention of killing the Arab. I said . . . that it was because of the sun." There was a gust of laughter, and now come the final bits of play acting, ballooning sleeves flicked back, jousts of eloquence between public prosecutor and defending counsel, and finally the verdict. "The presiding judge had already started pronouncing a rigmarole to the effect that 'in the name of the French People' I was to be decapitated in some public place." So are the tragedies the sun brings judged on the level of history, but on the level of history alone, that is to say, of man mutilated.

"Me not there." Under an empty sky empty men have passed sentence on emptiness. For us there remains only a memory of Meursault, a shallow saint. But there is no saint who hasn't a method and no saint who hasn't a message, and Camus leads his hero on to his heaven. A priest comes to see him in the condemned cell. What can he do to help him? Meursault has no conception of what sin is. He is only aware that he is guilty; they have told him so. What about God? "I explained that I didn't believe in God.

"'Are you really so sure of that?' "I said I saw no point in troubling my head about the matter; whether I believed or didn't was, to my mind, a question of so little importance." You mean there is nothing you know is true, nothing you are sure about? Well yes, there's the world around about us, that's solid enough. Just this world, and you haven't any wish for another life to come? Surely every thinking creature looks forward to a future life? Did he not? "Of course I did, I told him . . . But that had no more importance than wishing to be rich, or to swim very fast, or to have a better shaped mouth. It was in the same order of things. He cut in with a question: how did I picture my life after the grave? I fairly bawled out at him: 'A life in which I can remember this life on earth.'" All of a sudden Meursault cannot stand the priest's chatter any longer. Something cracks and he grabs him by the neck-band of his cassock, to pour out in his face all that has lain on his heart and this time "in a sort of ecstacy of joy and rage." Sure of anything? Oh yes, I'll tell you!

"He seemed so cocksure, you see. And yet none of his certainties was worth one strand of a woman's hair. Living as he did, like a corpse, he couldn't even be sure of being alive. It might look as if my hands were empty. Actually, I was sure of myself, sure about everything, far surer than he; sure of my present life and of the death that was coming. That, no doubt, was all I had; but at least that certainty was something I could get my teeth into—just as it had got its teeth into me. I'd been right, I was still right, I was always right. I'd passed my life in a certain way, and I might have passed it in a different way, if I'd felt like it. I'd acted thus, and I hadn't acted otherwise; I hadn't done x, whereas I had done y or z. And what did that mean? That, all the time, I'd been waiting for this present moment, for

45

that dawn, tomorrow's or another day's, which was to justify me. Nothing, nothing had the least importance, and I knew quite well why. He, too, knew why. From the dark horizon of my future a sort of slow, persistent breeze had been blowing towards me, all my life long, from the years that were to come. And on its way that breeze had leveled out all the ideas that people tried to foist on me in the equally unreal years I then was living through. What a difference could they make to me, the death of others, or a mother's love, or his God; or the way one decides to live, the fate one thinks one chooses, since one and the same fate was bound to 'choose' not only me but thousands of millions of privileged people who, like him, called themselves my brothers. Surely, surely he must see that? Every man alive was privileged; there was only one class of men, the privileged class. All alike would be condemned to die one day; his turn, too, would come like the others'. And what difference could it make if, after being charged with murder, he were executed because he didn't weep at his mother's funeral, since it all came to the same thing in the end? The same thing for Salamano's wife and for Salamano's dog. That little robot woman was as 'guilty' as the girl from Paris who had married Masson, or as Marie, who wanted me to marry her. What did it matter if Raymond was as much my pal as Céleste, who was a far worthier man? What did it matter if at this very moment Marie was kissing a new boyfriend? As a condemned man himself, couldn't he grasp what I meant by that dark wind blowing from my future? . . . '' They pull them apart, and the priest goes. Meursault gets calmer and flings himself on his bunk, exhausted. Night falls. When he woke, ''with the stars shining down on his face,'' Meursault, ''washed clean and emptied of hope,'' can now open his heart ''to the benign indifference of the universe.'' As they say, all's well that ends well. ''For all to be accomplished, for me to feel less lonely, all that remained was to hope that on the
46

day of my execution there should be a huge crowd of spectators and that they should greet me with howls of execration.''

This was the tale which left Camus' readers, in that difficult and unhappy period they were living through, with what you might call a hopeful pessimism. A little later, readers with time to pause and reflect could see the tender touches here and there. They recalled old Salamano and his mangy dog and the unceasing insults the ''stinking beast'' had to put up with, and how inconsolable the old man was when he lost his pet. ''Through the wall there came to me a little wheezing sound, and I guessed that he was weeping.'' It became clear to them who Camus was and what was the job he had been doing, and they saw in another light the description of the scene in court. ''The journalists had their fountain pens ready; they all wore the same expression of slightly ironical indifference, with the exception of one, a much younger man than his colleagues, in grey flannels with a blue tie, who, leaving his pen on the table, was gazing hard at me. He had a plain, rather chunky face; what held my attention was his eyes, very pale, clear eyes, riveted on me, though not betraying any definite emotion. For a moment I had an odd impression, as if I were being scrutinized by myself.'' The public at large also, as soon as the book appeared, made no mistake. They had of course no ears for the Vichy newspaper reviewer who spoke of ''sad sloppiness'' and ''the man who gave up,'' but also they did not share the view of some, like Jean Guéhenno, that a demonstration of the absurd was without utility. For *The Stranger* without any precaution in any single line of the text, was not a ''substitute for revolt'' but called it forth and strengthened it. With Vichy France in its full flood of ridiculous propaganda, *The Stranger* gave what was vitally necessary, the basic truth and a firm springboard. We could see that—at last!—we had a mature literature and that the writers who had not feared to take up the cudgels, though still condemned to a life mainly in the cellars—I mean Malraux, Mauriac, and Sartre—had been joined by a new man of obvious courage and responsibility who had created a tragic hero with the sole aim of helping men to meet and beat what they were having to put up with. It was stoicism and its grandeur, and no one could then foresee that so shortly after victory, or what was to be called victory, there would be men to demand bonfires for such works, in their haste to dig out the messages of Right and Left with which Fascists and Marxists had sought to delude.

In correct chronology, *Cross Purpose* is later than *Caligula* and *The Myth of Sisyphus,* in the matter of writing at least. If I have decided to deal with it next, it is because, rightly or wrongly, I regard it as a transition between the "clear-swept table" of *The Stranger* and the explosion of *Caligula* followed by the defining role of *The Myth,* and also because the subject of the play is already to be found in *The Stranger,* in Meursault's telling of his find in the prison. "One day, when inspecting my straw mattress, I found a bit of newspaper stuck to its underside. The paper was yellow with age, almost transparent, but one could still make out the print. It was the story of a crime. The first part was missing, but one gathered that its scene was some village in Czechoslovakia. One of the villagers had left his home to try his luck abroad. After twenty-five years, having made a fortune, he returned to his country with his wife and child. Meanwhile his mother and sister had been running a small hotel in the village where he was born. He decided to give them a surprise and, leaving his wife and child in another inn, he went to stay at his mother's place, booking a room under an assumed name. His mother and sister completely failed to recognize him. At dinner that evening he showed them a large sum of money he had on him, and in the course of the night they slaughtered him with a hammer. After taking the money they flung the body into the river. Next morning his wife

came and, without thinking, betrayed the guest's identity. His mother hanged herself. His sister threw herself into a well."

Meursault comments: "In one way it sounded most unlikely; in another, it was plausible." It could not be better put. In *Cross Purpose*, Camus does not seek to embroider on the plot. He takes it as he finds it. One could almost say it is a bequest from Meursault. He sees it as a piece of false pretense and therefore a subject highly suitable for the stage. For there is no better subject for a play than false pretenses, permitting a secondary action inside the main, with the author taking the public for his accomplice against the actors on the stage, the cast on puppet strings and the audience in the know. Here of course the swindler is fate. Camus logically breaks the story into three acts: (1) Jan's return; (2) his murder; (3) the revealing of the truth. All he adds is size to the protagonist, and this is not Jan but his sister Martha; and one member to the cast, Fate itself, in the person of an old dumb manservant.

When the play was put on at the Théâtre des Mathurins, in the excitable Paris of 1944, it met with a mixed reception; some began by being embarrassed before becoming frankly hostile and others were enthusiastic. There was argument after argument, the ill-disposed mainly attacking the play's technique and the defenders stressing the quality of the subject and dialogue. The dramatic logic of the play is not without contrivances, this cannot be denied; the whole action rests on a succession of chances. It is sheer luck that decrees that it is not a "happy ending." The suspense from Martha's hesitations—kill him, not kill him—the chances she keeps giving him to save himself which he does not take; the hesitations of Jan himself who again and again nearly lets out who he is; the entries and exits of his wife Maria who could let everything out of the bag but is perpetually doing everything at the wrong time, all these are elements of vaudeville, let us face it, and give the play a laughable side. Are we then to laugh? The audience in 1944 did not think so; they had been told they had a "serious" author. And yet, of course, we must laugh at *Cross Purpose,* not, if you please, with the automatic laughter touched off by gags and comic situations, but with the laughter of the connoisseur of life. In the end, that laughter is what life is made of. Our existence, "in one way unlikely, in another, plausible," turns on chances which are not a whit less fantastic than what we find in *Cross Purpose*; at any moment, a word, a gesture, someone dropping in, can put happiness in the balance or a spoke in the wheel of misfortune. "Anyhow, to my mind, the man was asking for trouble; one shouldn't play fool tricks of that sort," is Meursault's pitiless comment.

Jan himself tells us that he proceeds as he does in an endeavor to know better what he so much desires to get back, a mother and his country. Whom does he remind us of? Naturally, Gide's *Prodigal Son* whom Camus, you will recall, had put on the stage in Algiers. Only, it is his sister Martha, to whom he presents himself incognito, who has taken over the role of the younger son whom his brother's return drives into flight. She also dreams of a country, the far-off South, the sea, in other words, freedom, and she expects from the crime she mediates the funds she needs. This gives us the confrontation of two desires, two expectations, the man with his air of "complete innocence" and the harsh old maid bearing all the burden of frustrated impatience, her impatience to merge in the universal All and find there a "presence," like Patrice Meursault. This is an irreconcilable antagonism. He wants to stay and foster his acquaintance with people, his relatives, and "reach the depths of the known to know it thoroughly" (Claudel's accusation of Baudelaire), while his sister burns with desire for the unknown and the absolute. "JAN: Perhaps it is the same thing with some hearts; perhaps they would blossom if you helped them with your patience. MARTHA: I have no patience . . . No, I prefer to picture those other lands over which summer breaks in flame." Above them is the old serving man; anybody can call him whenever they like, but he appears only in mute silence. "The bell works but *he* doesn't speak."

Alea jacta est. Not having read the name on the passport which her brother hands her to put chance to the test (she only felt the weight of it), Martha puts poison in her brother's cup of tea. ("JAN: Anyway, I would like to thank you for the tea, and for the welcome you have given me. THE MOTHER: Really, sir, we have done very little for you. Being thanked for something due to a mistake is always embarrassing.") The next day the fateful passport has to be burned so as not to arouse the suspicions of the police. This time, of course, the name hits them in the eyes.

Exit the mother to find her death (how the silent mother and accomplice, doomed to a lonely death in home or well, pervades these early works of Camus!), and Martha is alone for a time on the stage, not freed as she had hoped but overwhelmed. "Let every door be shut against me. I hate this narrow world in which we are reduced to gazing up at God." Re-enter Jan's wife, Maria, to be told the news and receive a final message from the murderess. "So all of us are served now, as we should be, in the order of things. But fix this in your mind; neither for him nor for us, neither in life nor in death, is there any peace or homeland." Alone again, Maria drops to her knees. "Oh God, I cannot live in this desert! Have pity, turn towards me. Hear me and raise me from the dust, oh Heavenly Father! Have pity on those who love each other and are parted." The door opens, enter the old servant. With the first words he has uttered: "Did you call me? MARIA: Oh! ... I don't know. But help me, help me, for I need help. Be kind and say you will help me. THE OLD MAN-SERVANT (in a clear, firm tone): No."

Between *Cross Purpose* and *Caligula,* there is, most strangely, since the second was written before the first, undeniable progress in our dramatist. Camus no longer puts on stage irritatingly facile symbolic characters, his ideas are no longer "clamped" onto the text, and above all his hero exists, acting and not acted upon. For the vast

52

theater of the world, *Cross Purpose* has only one character, Fate. Caligula has invented his own theater.

It is 38 A.D. The young Emperor Caius Caligula, whose reign has begun in sweetness and light, has just lost his sister Drusilla to whom he was bound, as everyone knew, by bonds other than those of consanguinity. Her death seems to have reduced him to despair, he has left the palace and disappeared. The patricians are concerned. What is the use of an emperor with love sorrows? If they knew what was going on, they would be far more deeply concerned, for it is not the death of Drusilla that has hit Caligula like a bolt from the blue, it is death, simply death itself. It is the brutal revelation of "a childishly simple, obvious, almost silly truth" that Caligula, when he finally returns, confides to his freedman, Helicon. "Men die; and they are not happy." Is that all? "Anyhow, Caligula," Helicon rejoins, "it's a truth with which one comes to terms, without much trouble. Only look at the people over there. This truth of yours doesn't prevent them enjoying their meal." But Caligula says: "All it proves is that I'm surrounded by lies and self-deception. But I've had enough of that; I wish men to live by the light of truth." You want me to rest? "That's not possible, Helicon. I shall never rest again."

Never again, indeed Caligula must now have a thing which men are content to ask for as a joke, the moon. Since they ask for it only as a joke and since these great children know only how to resign themselves and laugh at it, he will be their teacher, for he has the means and he knows what he is talking about. The means, of course, are power. With a power called absolute, the young emperor will use it to fight on almost equal terms against the absolute of the absurd. Since everything is absurd on the higher level, he will create the absurd on the lower level, in other words, freedom. He will no more allow false

53

reasoning to paralyze men. "This world has no importance; once a man realizes that, he wins his freedom . . . Go and spread the news in Rome that freedom has been given her at last, and with the gift begins a great probation."

These are words full of foresight; a people has indeed a great probation before it when it has a superman on the throne. Not that we would insult Caligula by comparing him to Hitler, a hasty comparison some writers have made, for the young and handsome Caius, radiating epicene charm even in his evil-doing (or what we call so), is not to be put in the same class as a dull-witted killer with an *idée fixe* as uninspired as racism; he stands out in relief in a text from the pen of his creator: "I believe that, without letting up in our struggle against them, we have to understand the error of the ways of those who in an excess of despair have rushed to this or that nihilism of our times." Nevertheless, even turning his back on three wars as they boil up, even putting the words "victory" and "conquest" in quotation marks like all others, he too ends up in crime. But as an artist, of course. Murder considered as one of the fine arts is the logical consequence, and a pretty poor one, of his skirmish with the absolute. Kirilov could prove liberty only by killing himself. Caligula is to prove it only by killing others.

First victims on stage! and Caligula's strength of conviction is shown by our being the doting accomplices of his early crimes. When he decrees that, to bolster the Treasury, the well-off patricians are to disinherit their children, make wills in favor of the State, and then be eliminated straightway "on a list to be drawn up," for, "if the Treasury has paramount importance, human life has none," when he starts to despatch this and that senator stiff with feebleness or stupidity, even when he murders before our eyes old Mereia for having taken a remedy against asthma, we laugh, we agree, we admit along with
54

him that "all true passion has a spice of cruelty." (Well now! That's a rather disquieting thing to approve of, for, after all, even in the half-light of the theater and despite theatrical illusion, our great humanity should be shuddering, does it mean there are crimes that are permitted? We have proclaimed such virtuous indignation at the degrading of man, in concentration camps for instance, and we find ourselves laughing, we never fail to laugh, when Caligula takes his friends' wives for prostitutes or makes the senators run round his litter?) But before long the quest for freedom through the absurd arouses a revolt more powerful than the one that inspired the quest. The time comes when Caligula, even in the absolute, is wrong.

It is not long before two characters, Cherea the patrician and Scipio the poet, are opposing him, not for such mean reasons as saving their skins but in the name of a higher Order. Both of them, and this is their originality, understand Caligula and to a certain extent love him, but both, though penetrated with the truth which he has discovered—and they have approached it themselves with a certain degree of danger—would rather have the other truth with which they are inspired. Cherea sees quite clearly, he was born by chance, like you and me, into an absurd world, he has elected to live in it and for that will grant it a meaning, a coherence. "I like, and need, to feel secure." He admits it very humbly and (Caligula makes no mistake here) moderately: "What I want is to live, and to be happy. Neither, to my mind, is possible if one pushes the absurd to its logical conclusions. As you see, I'm quite an ordinary sort of man. True, there are moments when, to feel free of them, I desire the death of those I love, or I hanker after women from whom the ties of family or friendship debar me. Were logic everything, I'd kill or fornicate on such occasions. But I consider that these passing fancies have no great importance. If everyone set to gratifying them, the world would be impossible to live

55

in, and happiness, too, would go by the board. And these, I repeat, are the things that count, for me.'' Yes, all that is moderate, a matter of good social hygiene, and Cherea caps it (or decorates it?) with another sentence which puts us all on his side. ''Certainly I believe that some actions are more praiseworthy than others.''

Young Scipio for his part is a poet, and, suddenly, Caligula, the creator, finds himself face to face with another creator. Cherea, in the name of order, spurned the emperor's inhuman lyricism, but Scipio faces him with another lyricism, the lyricism of nature, of ''the harmony between one's feet and the earth.'' Scipio is well aware that death, whose showing has overwhelmed Caligula and which he flourishes as the explanation and excuse for all he does, is inherent in life, is life itself: ''the sky all flushed with red, wild, sweet, festal joys . . . '' He rises against the tyrant, not only because he has killed his father (a murder which, on the contrary, could have created a bond between them) but because, with dirty, useless, and sacrilegious deaths, he has soiled great Death which gives man his weight and measure. In any case, what exactly is Caligula trying to do? He is trying to offset the ''hatred and stupidity of the gods.'' But Scipio rejoins: ''Hatred does not compensate for hatred. Power is no solution. Personally I know only one way of countering the hostility of the world we live in. CALIGULA: Yes? And what is it? SCIPIO: Poverty.''

From now on, Caligula suffers the worst of fates, condemned to clowning. A creator no longer; an ''artist'' aping creation. Scene by scene he becomes the caricature of himself. Of the deep purity of the first evening when he approaches the dead body of Drusilla, touches it with his fingertips, appears to reflect, and turns and rushes out into the night and rain, of all this nothing remains. His wedding with freedom has become a grotesque coition. On boards from which sense has fled, a poor strolling player executes vague movements, paints his toenails, dresses up as Venus, and forces poor poetasters to lick their tablets clean; his face—for the end, of course, is concealed by the means—is now the expressionless face of the executioner. "Execution delivers and relieves. It is universal, fortifying, and just in its application as in its intentions." Very true, indeed. "We shall be forever guilty." But did he have to want the moon in order to be persuaded of it? Can anyone now save Caius? Only two loyal souls now stand by him, Helicon out of indifference and devotion, and Caesonia for love. "Don't you realize what it can be to live and love quite simply, naturally, in . . . in purity of heart?" But it is now too late.

Nonetheless it had been a wonderful dream and Caligula had almost got the moon. "It was last summer. I had been gazing at her so long, and stroking her so often on the marble pillars in the gardens that evidently she'd come to understand . . . She was coy, to begin with. I'd gone to bed. First she was blood red, low on the horizon. Then she began rising, quicker and quicker, growing brighter and brighter all the while. And the higher she climbed, the paler she grew, till she was like a milky pool. Slowly, shily she approached, through the warm night air, light as gossamer, naked in beauty. She crossed the threshold of my room, glided to my bed . . ." Dreams, dreams. "Fewer and fewer people round me . . . You decided to be logical, didn't you, poor simpleton? . . . The question now is: Where will that take you?" How could he not know it?

The conspirators have made their last-act entry, on time, all poor fools or men of the mob, save Cherea, but what matter? Caligula now has the ultimate secret: "Killing is not the solution," and Caesonia, with his strangling hands on his throat, echoes: "How can you call it happiness, this terrifying freedom?" There is nothing left for him to learn except living through death, "that emptiness

57

beyond all understanding, in which the heart has rest." He smashes the mirror reflecting his last laugh on earth and falls stabbed through and through, with the cry: "I'm still alive!"

Such was the end of Caligula, who compared himself to the plague, with a face full of blood and laughter. For a judgment of him, let us turn to Camus himself. "Caligula is a man led by the passion for life into a frenzy of destruction, a man disloyal to man through his loyalty to himself. No value is safe from his challenge. But if his truth lies in denying the gods, his error lies in denying men. He did not come to understand that you cannot destroy everything without destroying yourself. It is a tale of the most human and most tragic of errors."

I come at last to *The Myth of Sisyphus* or "Is a man to attempt to live?"

The world is an absurd one. Meursault, Martha, and Caligula have, I think, made that sufficiently clear, at least to minds of higher perception. There is nevertheless a subtle difference to which the novelist and playwright accord little attention, but the essayist owes it to himself to define it. "I said that the world is absurd but I was too hasty. The world in itself is not reasonable, that is all that can be said. But what is absurd is the confrontation of the irrational and the wild longing for clarity whose call echoes in the human heart . . . From the moment absurdity is recognized, it becomes a passion, the most harrowing of all."

What is the Absurd? It is "the denseness and the strangeness of the world," it is "sin without God. There can be no absurd outside the human mind. Thus, like everything else, the absurd ends with death. And it is by this elementary criterion that I judge the notion of the absurd to be essential and consider that it can stand as the first of my truths."

What is the escape from this prison? Of course there are

58

religions, but the author without hesitation will have none of them. Not only does he refuse to make the leap which they wish to force him to make but also he finds no interest in the promise or threat which necessitate it. "What comes after death is futile." Is it then to be suicide? Suicide has implacable logic on its side. Since silence is nature's response to man's anguish, man, "being undeniably plaintiff and respondent, judge and accused" (Dostoevsky), has the fullest right to condemn her also to go under with his loss of consciousness. This, as Camus rightly notes, is the approach of the "vexed" man. The case of Kirilov, it is true, contributes a higher reason. "If God does not exist, Kirilov is god. Kirilov must therefore kill himself to become god. That logic is absurd, but it is what is needed." Yet, it is not through such a negative gesture that man will raise himself to the dimension of the absurd. For "it is essential to die unreconciled and not of one's own free will. Suicide is a repudiation. The absurd man can only drain everything to the bitter end and deplete himself." On the contrary, it is through the lonely effort of an extreme and daily strain, by which we will give proof day by day to his only truth, which is defiance. "Living is keeping the absurd alive." A man must therefore live.

"I establish my lucidity in the midst of what negates it. I exalt man before what crushes him, and my freedom, my revolt, and my passion come together then in that tension, that lucidity, and that vast repetition."

Once he has made this profession of faith, careers in the absurd are opened to man. Camus sees at least three such, those of Don Juan, the actor, and the conqueror. All three—Don Juan refusing regret and hope, the actor who has chosen "multiple fame" and is the illustration of "that so suggestive truth that there is no frontier between what a man wants to be and what he is," and the conqueror who prefers action "without nostalgia or bitterness," to all else

—have, by virtue of the Absurd, "a royal power. It is true that those princes are without a kingdom. But they have this advantage over others: they know that all royalties are illusory." There is, however, one being who excels them all, and this is the being absurd par excellence, the creator. For he is in a situation of total contradiction. He admits that it is possible that his creation "does not exist." He works "for nothing," and knows that no future lies before his creation (for what is called posterity is a delusion even for the highest and greatest), he can see his works destroyed in a day and admit it is of no importance; but at the same time his conscience, enlightened and magnified by his works, remains constantly alive and constantly bears witness to the "brilliant and reasonless imagery of the world. To create is to give a shape to one's fate. In that daily effort in which intelligence and passion mingle and delight each other, the absurd discovers a discipline that will make up the greatest of his strengths." And straightway, myth hastens to illustrate that effort.

Sisyphus, having committed the unpardonable crime of being too much attached to the things of this world, was condemned by the gods to roll a rock endlessly to the top of a hill. It is a terrifying torture but the victim overcomes it through the certainty that his efforts, precisely, are hopeless. "The absurd man says yes and his effort will henceforth be unceasing." In this realization which should be his torment lies, on the contrary, his victory. "There is no fate that cannot be surmounted by scorn." In the end, with his face close to the rock and his hands cruelly grasping it, Sisyphus finds a joy unknown to the gods themselves. "He knows himself to be the master of his days. This universe seems to him neither sterile nor futile. Each atom of that stone, each mineral flake of that night-filled mountain, in itself forms a world. The struggle itself towards the height is enough to fill a man's heart. One must imagine Sisyphus happy."

Are we to find in *The Myth of Sisyphus,* as M. Henry Amer does, "a charter of atheistic humanism," or more simply "the tempting of a young man aware of the tragic of his time to exorcise the temptation to suicide and despair"? The question is less for Sisyphus than for his rock. Christians and, in rather less definite manner, the idealists, will not have it that the rock always comes back to the same place and claim that every effort of the man chained to it hoists it towards the summit and that one day Sisyphus will straighten his back, with his task accomplished, a man saved or a conqueror. If you imagine the contrary you accept tragedy, which many hold incompatible with happiness. "The abstract response of Sartre is in this more realistic than the generous strivings of Camus. A happy Sisyphus cannot really exist, he is a figment of the imagination" (José Orlandis). Let us pass on from these considerations to an image, the image, in fact, of a happy Sisyphus, my recollection of Camus himself at that time.

The Myth had been out for some months when I finally made the acquaintance of its author. It happened in circumstances which history makes memorable. There were a dozen of us, gathered one June evening at Charles Dullin's place, writers, journalists, actors (Simone de Beauvoir, Maria Casarès, Queneau, Salacrou, Sartre), and Sartre had brought Camus. The evening was prolonged into the night and there was a moment when the alert was sounded. When the morning was yet young we heard that the Allies had landed.

I still see Camus that night, while the news of the great event had still to reach us, and I recall an insistent jingle going round and round in my head for the first hour or two of our meeting. What would not leave me was the personal messages which London, as everyone will recall, was sending out to the Resistance: "The crocodile has sneezed on the carpet three times. Aunt Ursula's tea is perfumed with arsenic." The need for such messages was undeniable but they were nonetheless the symbol of the infantilism of war, of any war, and the hard lot of adult men condemned to play with weapons and words of puerile violence.

I watched Camus and, suddenly, a great contrast was clear to me, the contrast between that infantilism and the handsome, tender, serious face of Camus. There the absurd and here the calm challenge. I was still full of *The Myth* and what I had found in it and I little understood, I believe, what I must now set down at the close of this chapter: namely, that for Camus the absurd was only a starting point, that before long he would regret being caught in that formula, and that it was for him only "an idea picked up in the street of the time he lived in." Still, the face I saw made clear to me that Camus had explored the absurd only to be better able to seek out the *raison d'être* of each of us. Yes, from that moment and whatever the issue of the battle, of all battles, including the last which we always end by losing, victory was not in doubt. It would be won by this clear-minded man without fear and without hope. Against war. Against the absurd. Against the gods.

CAMUS THE MAN

Camus had in fact returned to France for reasons of health. In 1942 the landings in North Africa had cut him off from his family. The Gallimard publishing house, which had published *The Stranger,* engaged him as publisher's reader. In the meantime, Camus had become a member of the Resistance, operating first in Lyon and then in Paris.

One August morning, Paris awoke to find new newspapers being peddled in the faces of the last German occupants trapped in the capital. One of these papers,

carrying the cross of Lorraine, particularly attracted public attention. It was called *Combat,* like the resistance group, underground until a day or two before, of which it was the mouthpiece, and it printed as subtitle: De la Résistance à la Révolution. A stirring leading article on the front page called the Parisians to the liberation of their city. "Paris is shooting all her bullets in the August night. In this vast setting of stone and water, all around this river which has reflected so much history, the barricades of freedom have once more been thrown up. Once more justice must be bought with the blood of men."

The other newspapers, of course, printed a similar appeal, in different style. But the anonymous lead-writer of *Combat* was alone in this, that from the first day he had an eye to the morrow of the battle and the days to come. "This dreadful travail will give birth to a revolution. No one can hope that men who have fought in silence for four years and are now fighting all day long in the din of bombs and the crackle of guns will agree to the return of the forces of surrender and injustice under any circumstances." And he was also the only one not to forget, in the heat of battle, to repudiate violence for its own sake. "Time will bear witness to the fact that the men of France did not want to kill and that their hands were clean when they entered a war they had not chosen."

Twenty-four hours later, Leclerc's first tanks entered the capital. The lead-writer hailed the event and the unparalleled night." He did not forget the dead and their sacrifices. "Nothing is given to men, and the little they can conquer is paid for with unjust deaths. But man's greatness lies elsewhere. It lies in his decision to be stronger than his condition. But if his condition is unjust, he has only one way of overcoming it, which is to be just himself." The days went by, the same lofty tone was kept, but there was a change of subject. The way of the barricades was over, and here and there dissension was beginning to creep into the victorious camp. It was time to leave enthusiasm for criticism.

Malraux visiting Camus.

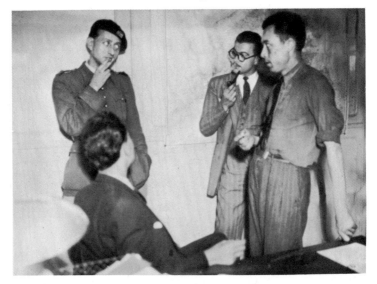

We cannot follow the lead-writer of *Combat* in all the struggles he entered into in 1944-1945. The drama of *épuration* was one of the first he had to give his attention to. He was in a difficult position, for on the one hand he wanted and demanded justice, a justice all the stricter for his not being able to see any available defending counsel outside this world, and on the other hand he refused to countenance a wholesale settlement of accounts under which a political operation very often lurked. The as yet unknown lead-writer had comrades not, indeed, to avenge but to justify in the public eye. There were the same difficulties, on a less elevated level obviously, in forming a view on, for instance, what the Communist Party was doing; Combat mistrusted its doctrines of efficiency at all costs, but could not sanction any anti-communism born out of bourgeois reaction. In all things moderation, in moderate tones. But not so at the opening of the Era of Fear: on the 8th of August 1945, the voice of *Combat* was once more raised alone, when it spoke of the bomb dropped on Hiroshima. "It can be said in a single sentence. Mechanical civilization has now attained in this act its lowest level of savagery."

But the lead-writer's favorite subject of polemics was the press itself and journalism. Here again he went straight to the essential point, for if the world had been in such bad shape and if, alas, the world was still not as well as could be desired, the primary cause was the lost conscience of its peoples, and, first and foremost, the futility of those appointed to inform them. Now as before, the sin of the press was sloth. It was getting rapidly farther and farther away from its duty, as laid down during the Resistance, of being "a press of courage and energy speaking in clear and respectable language." What had to be done now was to revise the values of journalism and raise its sense of responsibility. With this in view, and in order to give his country a voice that would be heard and would be and remain "the voice of energy rather than of hatred, proud objectivity and not rhetoric, humanity instead of mediocrity,'' the lead-writer was in favor of a real charter for the press. The guidelines he wished his confreres to accept (and, as a beginning, imposed in his own editorial office) were that they should inform well rather than inform quickly, bring out the meaning of each piece of news with an appropriate commentary, launch a reign of critical journalism, and never at any time allow politics to get the upper hand over morals nor let morals descend into moralizing. Himself conforming to these rules, he found himself—the truth will out—losing readers while the other papers, ignoring them, saw their circulations increase. In November 1944, when Metz was taken, the serious report in *Combat* rated low in public opinion in comparison with what the other papers had seen first and foremost, namely Marlene Dietrich returning to the city.

Nonetheless, there is no doubt about it, France has seldom had a newspaper to compare with *Combat* of that time for its discipline and style, the value of the news it carried, and its readers' respect. What, then, was this new newspaper, which its faithful readers read from the first word to the last? It was above all a team of friends housed in a requisitioned printing shop and with manners and ways far removed from those of "press magnates." For some time the administrative side, for instance, contrary to what happens in every newspaper in the world, was the poor relation of the editorial room. In the early days the money that came in from distributors, street-vendors, subscribers, etc., was simply chucked into a basket, and in the evening accounts were made up and it was shared out. And those working on this so unorthodox paper were men of its own stamp. The manager had a rooted horror of specialists and made no bones about keeping out of any department anyone who had made his career in that line, and put in men who knew little of it but would bring new eyes to the job. Thus Sartre, a philosopher, was put in

The staff celebrates the first number of *Combat* to be issued to a liberated Paris.

charge of reporting on the uprising in Paris, while Jacques Lemarchand, who seldom went to the theater, was given dramatic reviews and made a great name in that line. But such eccentricities were no longer a source of amazement, for the Parisian press was beginning to know Pascal Pia.

It was the same Pia, indeed. He had left Algiers, after the foreseeable demise, under Vichy, of *Alger Républicain* and its successor *Soir-Républicain* and, true to himself, had fought in the Resistance. Everything in his character made that inevitable, his patriotism and his liberalism, and even his partiality for hoaxes which turned out very useful for leading the Gestapo up the garden path. Pia managed

Combat, but he left editorial writing to another, his friend of the Algiers years 1937-1940, Albert Camus.

Camus the Algiers reporter lived on in Camus the lead-writer. For him the trade of journalist was as noble a one as that of novelist or dramatist; also the actual work of the printing shop was as important for him as any writing of articles. Roger Grenier, who saw these years through with him, gives us a picture of his friend "taking part in all discussions in the editorial room, checking copy, making headlines, and at the imposing table." He has noted Camus' preference for team work and his refusal to sign his leads, and has kept alive for us the picture of him, standing by the presses, watching the making-up, and the silent devotion of those around him. "All the administrative staff, all those in the printing shop, anyone who had any contact with him, even if they had not read his books or even, by taste or out of necessity, were far removed from the world of books, knew perfectly well who Camus was and were strengthened and enriched by being near him." After midnight, Camus finally left "his" newspaper, and it was then, though he never knew it, that the younger men on the editorial staff got themselves a galley-pull of his article and went off to an all-night cafe to read and discuss it.

A new man had come into the public eye; ask anyone and he would now be able to put a name and a face on the serious, anxious voice that rose above the hubbub of Liberation. People were beginning to know all about Camus, where he came from, what he had done during the dark years, and even about the painful illness which in 1942 had forced him to go to the department of Haute-Loire for treatment. They were well aware that he was the author of the *Letters to a German Friend* written under the Occupation "to throw some light on the blind battle we were then waging and thereby to make our battle more effective." I have said that in these *Letters* Camus makes a distinction between man and his temporary aberrations.

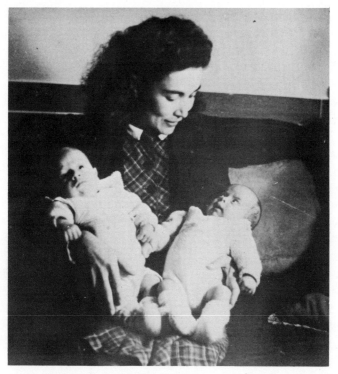

Francine Camus with the twins, Jean and Cathérine.

But he also had something to say about the victors as well. On heroism, for instance: "We profess it because ten centuries of history have given us knowledge of all that is noble. We distrust it because ten centuries of intelligence have taught us the art and blessings of being natural." In any case, "heroism is not much, happiness is more difficult." Camus again declares "I continue to believe that this world has no ultimate meaning," but he will not have it that this means taking refuge with the gods in the will to power. Against underlying despair, born of the great void of creation, he still holds that not all is permissible and "violence above all," but what Scipio opposed against Caligula: loyalty to the earth. "This world has at least the truth of man and what we have to do is to

69

forge reasons for him against fate itself. And the only reasons are man, and he it is who must be saved if the idea of life is to be saved. I see your contemptuous smile that says: How are we to go about saving man? I tell you with all the strength in me: it means not mutilating him, and it means giving justice, which man alone has conceived of," a chance.

Meantime, France was being born again and, having been saved by the strenuous endeavors of intelligence, was now giving herself up to the delights of intellectualism. Men of letters, with the credit of unbounded trust which their four years under censorship had earned them, were now in the limelight (and they had better enjoy it while they can; before long it will be the turn, again, of the whore and the warrior). Even the School of Algiers rose again and set out gaily to conquer Paris—their bookseller-publisher Charlot had come over—offering their sun-soaked metaphysics to the citizens of St. Germain-des-Prés. They encountered a formidable rival, the existentialist school under Jean-Paul Sartre and Simone de Beauvoir. Existentialism had quickly taken hold in Paris. Sartre had his regular table at the Café de Flore, and its proprietor, a man of Auvergne and of a school of avowed realists, shamelessly pointed him out to the gaping tourists, and the "little man" in thick glasses watched wave after wave of public curiosity breaking at his feet. Not that public curiosity was always well informed; the gapers were not very clear whether Existentialism was a new philosophy or a new style. Of course everything has already been said about that period when you expected poets and found professors turning up, when the soul at last could breathe in the fresh open air and bodies were in a hurry to go and skulk in cellars. One night at Tabou, which anyhow was not a cellar but a drinking-place, the muse of the locality, Mlle. Gréco, saw a tall dark young fellow in a blue shirt and raincoat. "Well, I never! He's dancing." And why shouldn't Camus be dancing?

Gérard Philipe rehearsing *Caligula* at the Théâtre Hébertot.

In point of fact, he didn't dance. By that I mean that the great post-war ballet couldn't get him to join in its constricted movements. The School of Algiers knew he had outgrown them and he would have nothing to do with existentialism, which he regarded as a "great adventure in thought leading to false conclusions." Whether he wanted it or not, he stood alone, with no illusions on the drawbacks his lonely stance would bring. For an eternal law was being borne out again, and the victors were donning the uniforms of the vanquished; after a long and terrible war for freedom, people were beginning to rediscover the advantages of the herd. There is seldom any room for the upright when "man is to be rescued" and the brigade is the order of the day, especially if your upright man is a writer of too recent fame which his confreres cannot stomach. And so, at the Café de Flore and in other places there began to be talk of "a prefabricated conscience" and "the man with his conscience between his teeth."

Some of their wounds had found a bit of soothing ointment, it is true, when *Cross Purpose* flopped, but it was

71

only a temporary respite. In 1945, at the Théâtre Hébertot, *Caligula* was a blaze of triumph. Truth and friendship require us to give a due share of the triumph to the man in the principal role, Gérard Philipe, a young actor still in the first stage of his career. Gérard Philipe's mad Caligula, calling down the moon, breaking the mirror, brought the audience to its feet. He was hardly more than 20. A teacher of elocution had once told him that his slightly nasal voice would keep him off the stage; on the contrary, it was the one defect to get an actor of genius out of the rut. And Philipe had genius. Lyrical, inspired, intelligent, he had all the gifts an actor required, together with features that were both handsome and expressive, tender and manly, and a body well attuned to the requirements of great parts. Moreover, his qualities as a man and above all his uncompromising honesty were on a par with his talents as an actor. Camus and Philipe became friends immediately. —I return to a photograph of that time in which Camus is in the wings watching Philipe rehearsing *Caligula;* there is such respect, admiration, and affection in his look! It is sickening to the heart to recall that the two were to die only a few weeks apart, fifteen years later. When he heard of Gérard Philipe's death and was told that he had directed that he should be buried without coffin, unguarded from the earth, Camus cried, "That's how I want to be buried too."

The triumph of *Caligula* came at a difficult moment, in the midst of the quarrel of the "philosophies of the absurd," which both Christians and Marxists accused of "copping out" from the service of mankind. The first blows had been delivered in the *Lettres Françaises* against Sartre, suddenly found guilty of bourgeois trends but actually intolerable to the Communist Party for being a Leftist but not a Stalinist. The phalanx was not long in joining the attack. The war cry rang out: Down with negative heroes! Long live the heroes who know what they want! "Should Kafka be burned?" was *Action's* question, answered by a downpour of partisan replies. Yes, burn Kafka and with him all the bringers of fear and uncertainty. How, we were asked, could fear exist in the light shone on us by Christ and Karl Marx, in a world in which you had merely to choose your camp? The "pessimists" among writers, those who would not have this too simple choice and refused this political tranquilizer, wanted moral and intellectual confusion. There was no mincing of words and labels; they were nihilists, reactionaries, Fascists in disguise.

Camus could not stand aside. Of course, he was not taken in. The intellectuals of St. Germain-des-Prés, in the shadow of their provincial church tower, might well think they were at the heart of the battle, but Camus knew that orders and blows came from another quarter, from party headquarters. Each of the parties, in the dawn of a Fourth Republic off to a poor start, strove to be the single party, to dictatorship. Full steam ahead, get the "lost sheep" back to the fold, and first and foremost those "peerers into the future" who would not believe that history could be shaped so easily. To this end, all means were proper: *l'Humanité* cried treason; *l'Aube* equated the philosophy of Nietzsche with secret indulgence in lechery and existentialism with contempt. With Kafka dubbed a corruptor, Nietzsche a hedonist, and Heidegger a buffoon, there was no reason not to string up symbolically—as a start— "despairing and discouraging" writers some of whom in truth had had a narrow shave with the real thing a year or two before. Camus lost no time in rebutting these lies. Briefly, in a few masterly lines, he put his finger on the main point. "We believe that the truth of this century can be reached only by going to the very end of its own drama. These times of ours have had their dose of nihilism and it is not by ignoring nihilism that we shall achieve the ethic we need." "It is a problem of civilization. We need to know whether man, unaided by the eternal or by rationalistic thought, can independently create his own values."

73

We know that "civilizations are not made by rapping people on the knuckles with a ruler. They arise from the confrontation of ideas, by the blood of the spirit."

It was not hard to see that what was at stake was liberty and justice, at a time which Camus saw was decisive. In an address which he gave at the Mutualité on the 15th of March 1945, when France fondly saw herself as a victim freed of her shackles, Camus, with a sheaf of facts to cite, denounced the persistence of lies and hate. His words come to us from a past which is already remote, over years of colonial wars, over an epoch in which France was a parody of the Resistance of 1940-1944, and they show us in advance how that parody would develop. "And perhaps the last and most long-lived victory of Hitlerism is to be found in the shameful scars made on the hearts of those who fought Hitlerism most vigorously." (Camus is here alluding to the ill-treatment and torture of "collaborators.") "The executioners' hatred engendered the vic-

Camus in the press box at the Pétain trial (second row, third from the left).

74

tims' hatred ... But that is simply giving in to the enemy ... Those poisoned hearts must be cured. And the most difficult battle to be won against the enemy in the future must be fought within ourselves, with an exceptional effort that will transform our appetite for hatred into a desire for justice ... It is essential, in short, to remake our political mentality ... It means that we must save intelligence ... There is no freedom without intelligence."

When Camus was speaking these words he knew that *Combat* was doomed sooner or later. The entertainment press had won the game; its readers were amused by the picturesque wine scandals but were indifferent to the real scandals, the "collaborator" lynched at Dijon with his eyes put out by a child of fourteen, the profiteers of the occupation period protected and relaunched into new business affairs, the rebels in Madagascar murdered by the thousands with the consent of a Christian pro-consul. Soon *Combat,* financially weakened, would be lost to its founders. It was at the mercy of an incident, a printers' strike which came in the spring of 1947. *Combat* in other hands, a newspaper "just like the other," in a word, without Camus, this was a sign; another page had been turned. Liberation was over. The Resistance had won but the Revolution was unaccomplished. Was there, among the writings of the time, a single work to carry it on? Sartre was losing himself in the labyrinth of *Roads to Freedom,* which in the end was to remain unfinished. His *Men Without Shadows,* he himself acknowledged, was nothing more than a tragic anecdote. Simone de Beauvoir's *The Blood of Others* dealt with only one point in the struggle, responsibility in face of the sacrifices of others. What did these works suffer from? Quite certainly, lack of perspective, the artist's own stepping back to synthesize the event and lift it into the higher category of fable. In short, what the Resistance was waiting for was a real work of art. We were waiting for a writer with a deeper intuition than the rest who could step back from recent events, could bring them into an allegory throwing light on history, could transport the years in time and space and thereby make them recognizable by any generation. What was wanted was chronicle and legend, the realistic and surrealistic, sun and history.

We were not disappointed. In 1947 came *The Plague,* an historic . . . and prophetic fable.

Oran. Look closely, but hurry, before long it will be a city closed to the world. Before long it will be the capital of disorder and horror.

But away with the images that Oran calls up. The story of *The Plague* takes place in the 1940's, not in the 50's or 60's as you might be tempted to think. The city in itself had not changed, not before the catastrophe hit it, and it was still the same as Camus had left it. Let us look through Camus' eyes at this future capital of the plague. It was an "ordinary place, treeless, glamorless, soulless," and Camus gives it four pages of almost exclusively negative description, as if he saw not so much the people, buildings, and walls as the void they stand in and the expectancy that rings them. Expectancy of what? Of death, of course. But dying in Oran means, or rather meant, simply ceasing to live. You had an existence with no future, an existence made up simply of habits, work, bathing, card games, and gossip, without the slightest "inkling of something different," for Oran is far and away the "town without intimations" and therefore "completely modern"—and then you went over without fuss out of being into non-being, in the discomfort of a dry climate. What was it the city lacked? It lacked precisely the sense of death, but this would appear "on the morning of 16 April" with the plague-ridden rats pouring out of the sewers and dying in the middle of the street. Suddenly, with the swarm of rats, which no one until then would admit existed, death ceases to be a habit like any other. It also ceases to be a habit of other people. It becomes "the concern of all of us." It becomes a tragedy.

If we have a tragedy, let us look at the cast. It will not take long for us to see that in fact it is a cast with one member, one only. But for the time being we will do as if the apparent number were real. There is Dr. Bernard Rieux who came upon the first dead rat on that April morning. He is about 35, medium build, always bareheaded, and "looks knowledgeable." He was born in a working-class family and had become a local general practitioner and lives with his old mother and his wife who has just been exiled to a sanatorium in France by a fatal illness. We note that in carrying out his duties as well as in his relations with his neighbors and confreres he can never get away from "a certain air of reserve" which people naturally take for indifference. Rieux belongs to those who believe "that the thing is to do your job as it should be done." His battle, devoid of all glamor, is on a very everyday level; he believes in doing something which is of immediate utility. What are we to think of a doctor who tells the wife of a patient simply "He's dead"? Only that he has nothing in his heart or that he has a secret. Rieux's secret is that he has never been able to stomach his powerlessness in face of the death of his fellow man and his air of reserve is his protest against a senseless universe whose ordainer is absent and in which the creatures suffer blindly and hopelessly.

A man with a secret, that is also the case of Jean Tarrou but he takes no pains to hide his mysteriousness. Tarrou is "a stocky, youngish man with a big, deeply furrowed face"; one day he appeared in Oran and no one knew where he came from or why. He does no work and lives by himself, spends his time strolling, bathing, watching the townspeople and keeping track of their idiosyncracies. And what is behind all this? A horrifying episode. His father was a man of the law and called for death sentences. He was a purveyor of the scaffold. The day Tarrou understood (at a trial his father had invited him to), the day he knew why, this or that morning, his father got up early in obedience to an alarm clock, Tarrou fled. He felt "pestiferous." The question of the death sentence apparently continued to pursue him, for he ran into an execution by shooting in Hungary. From that time his life was a horror but also an unshakable determination. "So that is why I resolved to have no truck with anything which, directly or indirectly, for good reasons or for bad, brings death to anyone, or justifies others' putting him to death."

The secret of Joseph Grand is a much more modest one. Joseph Grand, 50 years of age, working in the town hall for a pittance, deserted by a wife tired to death of his mediocrity, lives only to go home each evening and plunge into a novel of which he has not been able to write more than the first lines. "One fine morning in May a slim young horsewoman might have been seen riding a glossy sorrel mare along the flower-strewn avenues of the Bois de Boulogne." A hundred times the sentence is put back on the loom and a hundred times Joseph Grand, a Sisyphus toiling at the writing desk, sees how far he still is from the gift of perfect expression which one day will cause a dumbfounded publisher to exclaim: "Hats off, gentlemen!" As for the fourth member of the cast whom we have to mention, there is no secret about him, or hardly any. Raymond Rambert is a young journalist come to Oran for a reporting job which has fallen through; his only thought is to get back to Paris and his mistress. Love and happiness are the whole content of his life.

There we are, someone reaches for a bell-push, the curtain goes up, and the infected rats are all over the town. As was to be expected, the reaction is skepticism. In the middle of the twentieth century an epidemic like the plague could not break out in a modern city like this! So they say, but what they don't know is that the emptiness of life in Oran, a peace that is useless or, more exactly, unused, has in fact called up the plague. The inhabitants were not even aware of the happiness of dying. There it is, with buboes and death-rattle, nothing could be clearer. So they play with words. It is not the plague, only an ordinary malady, a "fever." But what about the rats? "One doesn't talk of rats at table," is Judge Othon's stern reply to his children. "We tell ourselves that pestilence is a mere bogey of the mind, a bad dream that will pass away. But it doesn't always pass away and, from one bad dream to another, it is men who pass away, and the humanists first of all, because they haven't taken their precautions." The health committee finally meets at the prefecture and those in authority do their best to push realities aside. When old Dr. Castel, a friend of Rieux, utters the fateful word, the prefect starts and automatically turns to the door as if "to make sure it had prevented this outrageous remark from being overheard in the passage." Oran may lull its anxieties with a harmless fever, but the world outside, still free of the scourge, knows exactly what is the word to put on it, and, one morning, the town is declared in quarantine. A state of siege is proclaimed and Oran is now a closed vessel. It is the beginning of the "intolerable leisure" which is the lot of dispossessed peoples cut off by the pitiless victory of evil. "We must conjure up once more those dreary evenings, sifting down through a haze of dust and golden light upon the treeless streets filled with teeming crowds of men and women. For, characteristically, the sound that rose towards the terraces still bathed in the last glow of daylight, now that the noises of vehicles and motors—the sole voice of cities in ordinary times— had ceased, was but one vast rumor of low voices and incessant footfalls, the drumming of innumerable soles timed to the eerie whistling of the plague in the sultry air above, the sound of a huge concourse of people marking time, a never-ending, stifling, drone that, gradually swelling, filled the town from end to end, and evening after evening gave its truest, mournfullest expression to the blind endurance which had ousted love from all our hearts."

There are two, however, for whom the plague is not entirely an ill wind, though for different reasons. Cottard, a curious fellow, had tried on the eve of the outbreak to commit suicide because of a vague accusation weighing on him, but now finds a new savor in life when he sees his fellow citizens' existence threatened. His "overfill of despair" rushes him into a phase of nihilism which he manages to turn to advantage (there are others who feel cheered up because everything is going wrong). The second is Father Paneloux, an eloquent Jesuit, who sees the plague as a punishment, the working of justice. From his cathedral pulpit, he points at a congregation which has gathered in the cathedral because "'anyhow, it can't do any harm,'" an accusing finger which brings them to their knees. "Calamity has come on you, my brethren, and, my brethren, you deserved it. Too long this world of ours has connived at evil, too long has it counted on the divine mercy." We can guess the rest, we know that, while we have here two, the "collaborator" and the mystic, who are resigned, the resisters are going to join up in a body, and this means a sanitary group. For "a fight must be put up, in this way or that, and there must be no bowing down."

This coming together, it is already clear, is effected in one single person. Whether it is Rieux or Tarrou, or even Joseph Grand and Rambert, it is Camus himself we see. He has Rieux's long-suffering humility in face of the daily task and his protesting reserve (as well as the old mother and a working-class father); with Tarrou he shares a taste for solitude, for detached roamings, sea-bathing, an instinct for observing, and opposition to the death penalty;

the unhappiness of Grand's passion for authorship humorously reflects his own fight as a writer for perfect expression; finally (and there is a small thing not to be forgotten,
namely, a report on *the state of the Arabs,* a continuation
piece to the *Kabylia Inquiry),* is it Rambert or Camus who
heads a list of noble values with love and happiness? And
which of the two do we hear saying: "Personally, I've seen
enough of people who die for an idea. What interests me is
living and dying for what one loves." This is an astounding
work built of all a writer's convictions, contradictions, and
temptations, in which we see him reflected in at least four
mirrors. But what we must admire here is that the
principle of "Know thyself" so clearly brings out all his
reasons for doing things at the same time as it does full
justice to his reasons for doing nothing. Rieux, having
known the school of "suffering"—another point of
resemblance with Camus—has learned at his patients'
bedsides how vain are "the never-lasting" victories;
he knows that the plague can only mean a "never-ending
defeat," but he also knows that man demands that the
endeavor shall be made to save him. Tarrou comes to help
him in the name of his "code of morals," "comprehen-
sion," but still with an *arrièrepensée;* he cherishes an
ambition, the ambition of becoming a saint outside faith
and churches. "Can one be a saint without God?—that's
the problem, in fact the only problem, I'm up against
today." Joseph Grand, for his part, who for the narrator
is, "more than Rieux or Tarrou" (this is to be noted) "the
true embodiment of the quiet courage that inspired the
sanitary groups," has no other ambition than the militant's
"'Plague is here and we've got to make a stand, that's
obvious. Ah, I only wish everything were as simple!'"
When we come to Rambert, it looks as if Camus enrolled
him in the Resistance only with burning regrets. He is an
unremitting would-be deserter and does everything to get
out of the city he is trapped in and back to the woman he

loves. He is without any hypocrisy and gives his friends his reasons quite unvarnished, and they approve. How could they not approve? If the happiness of men is their aim, must they not admit that, in the midst of the battle, a flag of happiness, ardently borne aloft and jealously guarded, justifies the warriors' being there and fighting? Yet, day after day, with all his stubborn attempts to get through the gates, Rambert feels a mysterious force keeping him a prisoner in the city. In the end he understands that "it may be shameful to be happy by oneself," and joins the sanitary group. "Until now I always felt a stranger in this town, and that I had no concern with you people. But now that I've seen what I have seen, I know that I belong here whether I want it or not. This business is everybody's business."

The dice are down. To the logical temptation to suicide Sisyphus had answered: Live and let live the absurd; against Caligula's nihilism Cherea sets the need of order in human things. The band of friends in *The Plague* meet the evil that faces them with union and fellowship. We need not go into the details of a tale everyone knows nor speak further of the faithful transposition, in the manner of Defoe, of the events of the occupation. "It is as reasonable to represent one kind of imprisonment by another, as it is to represent anything that really exists by that which exists not!" (This was quoted on the title-page of the work.) Inside the hell that Oran has become, where "men were killed off like flies," the drama, make no mistake, is in the souls of men. It is the drama of a band of brothers who find their motives in themselves alone, without any reference to a higher command or any absolute good. Men have undertaken to save other men, but they have no time for the ideal which alone would give a total meaning to their acts. They have no faith, but at least they have a conviction. This being so, they are higher and better than Father Paneloux, for instance, whose fierce belief soon

82

begins to weaken. Before his eyes a child lies dying, a death not to be justified. "Paneloux gazed down at the small mouth, fouled with the sores of the plague and pouring out the angry death-cry that has sounded through the ages of mankind. He sank onto his knees, and all present found it natural to hear him say in a voice hoarse but clearly audible across that nameless, never-ending wail: 'My God, spare this child.'" The child was not to be saved and for the first time Paneloux perceives the truth of another cry, the cry Rieux spits in his face: "'Ah! That child, at least, was innocent—and you know it as well as I do!'" Vainly, from now on, he seeks refuge in that grace which allows us "to love what we cannot understand." In vain also he takes a heroic part in the quite earthly battle of the sanitary groups. Even in that, he will always be an outsider, the doctrinaire who, through his submission to a will that is not to be understood, remains, for all the purity of his actions, in hidden complicity with evil. For Camus *The Plague* was his most anti-Christian work. He was certainly right in thinking so. *The Plague* tells the story of a fight not only waged and won without God, but finding its justification in itself alone. "Salvation," says Rieux, "is much too big a word for me, I don't aim so high. I'm concerned with man's health; and for me his health comes first." And, in clearer terms, "I have no idea what's waiting for me, or what will happen when all this ends. For the moment I know this: there are sick people and they need curing . . . Since the order of the world is shaped by death, might it not be better for God if we refuse to believe in him, and struggle with all our might against death, without raising our eyes towards the heaven where he sits in silence?"

This is a rejection of God, but to balance it there is a deep sense of the sacred, expressing itself in all that borders on the inexpressible, first of all exile, and the rest of the country, unreachable but ever-present with which there is no communication except by means of childish codes which lead to misunderstandings. It is at this point that Camus' transposition is at its most subtle and impressive. For if, between 1940 and 1945, the "rest of the country" meant the free nations, prosperous and happy, in *The Plague* it means simply and soley the main thing, love. Liberation has the features of love, the features of each of the women, the wife of Rieux dying in a far-off sanatorium, Rambert's mistress made insanely desirable by the distance separating them, even the old wife of Dr. Castel who comes back to join her husband and help him to face the plague which they regard as "insignificant" compared with being separated. We see here bitter, desperate desire, "a love that weighs heavy, an inert mass within us, sterile" but acute and unsatisfied also, and it is the real driving force of the fight against evil. Between Rieux and Tarrou there springs up a relationship of manly tenderness. "Do you know what we now should do for friendship's sake? Go for a swim . . . Tarrou was coming up with him, he now could hear his breathing. Rieux turned and swam level with his friend, timing his stroke to his. They dressed and started back. Neither had said a word, but they were conscious of being perfectly at one, and that the memory of this night would be cherished by them both." Towards the end of the book, Tarrou—the city's last case—is struck down by the pitiless sickness. We see, as we could have seen as twilight descended on a hard battle fought side by side, how Rieux the victorious knight, bends over his stricken companion, a fallen knight dying at the foot of a tree, and "this human form, his friend's, dying with a short, hollow groan," leaves him "on the shore, empty-handed, unarmed, and helpless." Rieux feels "that this defeat was final, the last disastrous battle that ends a war and makes peace itself an ill beyond all remedy."

The brotherhood knew it well, there are no victors. Of

course, one fine morning, after the death of the plague and the return, so early, of carefree foolishness, "the ceremonial opening of the gates took place, acclaimed by the populace, the newspapers, the wireless, and official communiqués." Everything takes its course as was to be foreseen, dancing on the public square, bouts of gluttony and boozing, and punishment for the horrible Cottard. But there is one man at least who is not taken in, and this is Rambert, by good luck safe and sound and now to be joined by his young mistress. "If only he could put the clock back and be once more the man who, at the outbreak of the epidemic, had had only one thought and one desire: to escape and return to the woman he loved! But that, he knew, was out of the question now; he had changed too greatly. The plague had forced on him a detachment which, try as he might, he could not think away." On the station platform, "he hadn't time to see her running towards him; already she had flung herself on his breast. And with his arms locked around her, pressing to his shoulder the head of which he saw only the familiar hair, he let his tears flow freely, unknowing if they rose from present joy or from sorrow too long repressed; aware only that they would prevent his making sure if the face buried in the hollow of his shoulder were the face of which he had dreamed so often, or, instead, a stranger's face. For the moment he wished to behave like all those around him who believed, or made-believe, that plague can come and go without changing anything in men's hearts." There is no doubt about it: Rambert will never again be truly happy.

Nor will Rieux, and this is not because he had lost a friend and a wife. "This chronicle is drawing to an end, and this seems to be the moment for Dr. Bernard Rieux to confess that he is the narrator." Are we finished with the book and its first person singular which told the tale for all those who could have told, the single one made plural

85

without visible effort by the working of an admirable novel technique, are we finished with our narrator ever absent and present like war and death themselves? No, we are not; already the doctor, stethoscope in hand, is bending over his first post-plague patient. What has he harvested from the great adventure? Little enough. He analyzes his reasons for telling the story, and all he finds are very modest ones, such as "not to be one of those who hold their peace but bear witness in favor of these plague-stricken people." To their greatness, their clear-sightedness, and their heroism? No, not that, but "to the injustice and outrage done them." Now less than ever has Rieux any illusions. He knows that no sovereign good can come of so much evil. Tarrou, who wanted to be a saint without God, only found his peace in death. All those who attempted to be higher and better than men while an inhuman tragedy was unfolding have found no answer. "These people were 'just the same as ever'" and their story must be reduced to a series of events acting on them without making any change in them. And yet, when this unrelenting analysis is over, there shines out a realization to which the plague has led Rieux, a humble truth of small dimension but not to be disdained, one which will light his path until the end of his days, that "there are more things to admire in men than to despise." That is enough, if one cannot be a saint, to help you to endeavor to be a doctor.

"And, indeed, as he listened to the cries of joy rising from the town, Rieux remembered that such joy is always imperilled. He knew what those jubilant crowds did not know but could have learned from books; that the plague bacillus never dies or disappears for good; that it can lie dormant for years and years in furniture and linen-chests; that it bides its time in bedrooms, cellars, trunks, and bookshelves; and that perhaps the day would come when, for the bane and enlightenment of men, it aroused its rats again and sent them forth to die in a happy city."

Sectioned into five long chapters, as classical tragedy traditionally falls into five acts, *The Plague* partakes of the nature of tragedy. It did not bear the word "novel" on its front cover; Camus disdained the commercial value of the word. He knew that he had written a dramatic chronicle, you might say a play between the covers of a book. Hence its greatness and its success. It is consequently surprising that in his following work Camus committed the mistake he had hitherto skillfully avoided of materializing allegory and putting it on a real stage, with loss of effectiveness.

Of course, the subject of *State of Siege* shows notable differences from that of *The Plague*. The action takes place in Cadiz, with the protagonist a tyrant of flesh and blood, seizing control of the city, installing a bureaucratic reign of terror, and yielding only when a hero revolts against the fear he had been a prey to. Yet *Plague* is the name of the tyrant and *Death* that of his secretary. The fact is that *State of Seige*, if it was not commissioned, did at least answer a demand. Jean-Louis Barrault had long had the ambition of putting Defoe's *Diary of the Plague Year* on stage. Knowing that Camus was writing a book on the same theme (and even prominently citing part of Defoe's text), he eagerly asked him to make an adaptation for the stage. Why an adaptation? Camus had transposed Defoe, what had he to gain from coming back to him again? And yet the theater attracted him and so did the show which Barrault, the sponsor of "total theater," put forward, not "a play of traditional structure but a spectacle with the acknowledged ambition of bringing together all forms of dramatic expression, from lyrical monologue to collective theater via miming, simple dialogue, and chorus." It was a partial revival of the medieval mystery or, rather morality play, shall we say *Tyranny Condemned* following on *Banquet Condemned*. In the end Camus agreed, perhaps not appreciating the prime requirements of the undertaking; it would call for art for the masses and the open air and require of the public a naivety which would not go with the plush and gilt of the Théâtre Marigny.

What also helped to decide him was probably the feeling that not all had been said in *The Plague* or rather the certainty that, a year having gone by, there was another *Plague* to be written and that this time the epidemic would have to have a name. The war had been over for three years and already totalitarianism was raising its head again. Yes, the times when "everything was so simple," as Joseph Grand would say, were far away. Now, former political deportees, like David Rousset, hardly back from Nazi camps, were denouncing other worlds of "concentration"; the Iron Curtain had slammed down and from behind it we had echoes of new trials and new executions. Between 1940 and 1945, everyone had seen the hangmen on the one side and the victims on the other. Now we were entering the Era of Suspects and everybody was *a priori* guilty, with the sole statement on that guilt losing itself in the emendations of history dictated by the dialectic of the leader, the party, and their executants, the bureaucrats of the reign of terror.

"We shall be forever guilty," you will recall, was the cry we heard from Caligula. And today it is what the tyrant Plague, the magician manipulator of history, announces from the walls of Cadiz to the city's inhabitants. He reigns, which is a fact and a right. His palace is a barracks, his hunting lodge a courtroom. Does he really govern? No, he functions. He brings organization. Fate is rational from now on, it occupies his offices. By means of health and life certificates arbitrarily issued or denied, everyone is kept track of statistically and placed in order for death under the whip of a master who has a horror of differentness and absurdity. Power was seized in the simplest manner you would conceive. Death, the tyrant's companion, wiped out with a simple stroke of the pencil anyone who rebelled. You cannot resist fear.

But you can. Among the terrified citizenry there is a young man called Diego; we shall not be surprised to learn that he is sensuous and in love, and at first quite taken up with the quest for happiness. There are certain rigidities in the constants Camus observes. Just as in *The Plague,* we have here a judge as the living representation of the old, bourgeois, and pseudo-liberal order, built of course on injustice; as in *The Plague,* couples are torn apart (by order of the tyrant); the "collaborator" Cottard, raised to a dimension of Caligula, is here the nihilist Nada (Nothing), the drunkard cripple to whom the Chorus sings a contradiction which could come straight from Cherea: No, it gives no justice, but it sets limits, and, lastly, as Martha in *Cross Purpose* dreamed of escape to the sea and Rieux and Tarrou in an evening swim slipped the chains of the epidemic, it is the cry "To sea! to sea!" which rouses the mad hopes of the oppressed population in *State of Seige.* But back to Diego again. As soon as his happiness is threatened he begins by seeking selfish protection; against death which is on his heels even in the house of his beloved he takes for his shield an innocent child, the son of his father-in-law-to-be. Thereupon revolt revolts against itself. A gesture not seen before must be found, but what is it to be? It comes to Diego instinctively when the secretary Death appears before him to mock him: he slaps her face. Sensation! The marks of condemnation he bears on his own flesh are wiped off by the blow that has been given. For there is a secret crack in tyranny's machine, all its power falls from it when it is faced by a man without fear, and now the only task is to snatch away the city's gag of fear. Diego leads the work; it costs him his life, but Plague is driven out. And the play ends with a Hymn to Liberty, and I shall not need to say which of the elements it is in which that hymn merges.

Cross Purpose had been a relative failure, and *State of Siege* was a complete flop, partly for the reasons I have

89

mentioned. Every musician must begin by having an instrument, and Camus had neither an ancient nor a medieval theater nor the unanimous audience of other times. (It would be interesting to put the play on again in the open air, as originally planned). We will not cast stones at the Parisian critics, for Camus had, too much, put strict adherence to the myth in front of the credibility of the characters, and these, let us face it, were not creatures of flesh and blood. It was written, however, that around 1950 his theater endeavors would see the pendulum swing and, on the 15th of December 1949, on the stage of the Théâtre Hébertot where Caligula had triumphed, *The Just* brought him back into public favor. A new step forward was being taken and the author was dealing now not only with rebellion but with its methods and actions. You can fight an epidemic or a tyrant, but with what arms? How is it to be done without giving pledges, without becoming Plague yourself, without denying yourself at the very time you are fighting?

History had an answer to these questions, to be found in one of its least-known chapters. Camus went to find the theme of *The Just* in the earliest years of this century; it deals with a small group of Russian terrorists who carried out bomb-attacks round 1905 under the cover of the Combat Organization of the Revolutionary Socialist Party. In his next work Camus was to give these very young terrorists, students for the most part, a name which could appear ironical, calling them "fastidious murderers." Kaliayev and his friends indeed lived a life of paradox. They had chosen the trade of assassin; nothing pushed them. They considered that revolution could make progress only through justice-dealing bombs. But at the same time they would not legitimate the means they were employing, avowed themselves guilty of bloodshed, were it even the blood of guilty men, were it even to promote the happiness of mankind. They required their own lives to pay for the lives they robbed of others. "Murder appeared to them as necessary and inexcusable."

As the curtain goes up, five terrorists, Dora Dulebov, Boris Annenkov (the leader of the group), Ivan Kaliayev, Stepan Fyedorov, and Alexis Voinov have decided to kill Grand Duke Serge while his carriage follows a carefully studied route. Kaliayev has been chosen to throw the bomb and the choice of Kaliayev is not to the liking of Fyedorov who regards Kaliayev, a poet and in love with Dora, as "too eccentric to be a revolutionary"; he is a man who asks himself too many questions, sees too clearly the differences between people and thereby, in spite of himself, does justice to part of the enemy front. Stepan for his part long ago stifled any questionings. The lashes he received in prison have justified him once for all, and he is now only a killing machine. Events, it appears, prove him right. At the instant the carriage passes within his reach, Kaliayev sees two unforeseen occupants, the nephew and niece of the Grand Duke whom he had taken along. The bomb is not thrown. Killing children, in Kaliayev's view, is not part of his mission.

The chance of an attack thrown away, delay accepted and a grave risk taken with his eyes open, an accusation of cowardice round his neck, nothing of all this could bring Kaliayev to strike at innocent children, even if the guilty should die alongside them. He is therefore himself a guilty man as he appears again before his friends and faces the anger of Stepan. The quarrel that arises is fundamental; when thousands of Russian children are dying of hunger, is their liberation to be put off by sparing the Grand Duke's well-fed nephew and niece? If so (this is Stepan speaking), "indulge in charity, and cure each petty little suffering as it comes along, but don't meddle with the revolution, which exists to cure all suffering, now and in the future." "But" (this is Dora's reply) "killing the Grand Duke's niece and nephew won't prevent a single

91

child from starving. Even destruction has a right and a wrong way and there *are* limits." "There are no limits!" shrieks Stepan, "all right is on the side of the revolution." A protest from Kaliayev: "I am ashamed of myself, Stepan, but I can't let you go on. I am ready to kill to overthrow the tyranny, but behind your words I see the threat of another kind of tyranny . . . and if ever it comes into power, it will make me a murderer! It's justice I try to fight for!"

That indeed is the problem, and the Organization, speaking through the mouth of the good and wise Annenkov, approves Kaliayev. "Killing children is a crime against a man's honor, and if the revolution should ever break with honor . . . then I should break with the revolution." Moreover, the attack is to be made all the same and this time Kaliayev sees it through. But the worst trial is in store. Kaliayev has been arrested after killing the Grand Duke and, of course, condemned to death. A surprising visitor is announced to him in his cell, it is the widow of his victim. Needless to say, an infamous calculation lies behind this development (the chief of police will use it to say that Kaliayev has repented and entreated for a pardon); however, it is the Grand Duchess herself who with the greatest sincerity in the world comes to ask for a pardon for Kaliayev. Inspired by pure Christian feelings she forgives her husband's murderer and wants to prolong his life in order that God may save his soul.

It is a terrible confrontation. Now more than ever Kaliayev puts his finger on the strange ambiguity of rebellion, innocent but never quite, striking down the guilty who are never quite guilty. "Do you know what he was doing two hours before he died? He was sleeping . . . in an armchair, with his feet up—he often used to do that. He was sleeping . . . and *you* . . . you were waiting for him in the cruel twilight." But the pity which assails him in this hour of doubt itself at the same time affords him his real salvation. Kaliayev refuses the pardon offered and in so doing justifies his action. Man against man, blood against blood—yes, he is truly a just man who accepts the obligation of killing for a cause on the sole condition of dying in turn. We see joined in Kaliayev the love of life and the vocation to suicide which so astonished Fyedorov. So he will die and his comrades, far from feeling themselves betrayed, will understand and admire the stand he has taken. Dora is the first to demand to follow his example, she will throw the next bomb and be the next for execution. "Don't cry, no, no, don't cry. Don't you realize that today is the day of our justification. Something has been born today which is our testimony, the testimony of us revolutionaries. Yanek is no longer a murderer! A horrible thud! That's all it took . . . one thud and he was plunged back into the joys of childhood! Do you remember his laugh? He used to laugh sometimes . . . for no reason at all . . . How young he was! He's laughing now . . . I know he is, his face pressed to the earth."

The responsibility of the Rebel and the return to innocence through the just counter-stroke of death are subjects to which Camus will turn again with passionate interest. Speaking of the terrorists he had just brought onto the stage, he was to say: "The extremists forgot nothing. A life is paid for by another life, and from these two sacrifices springs the promise of a value. Kaliayev and the others believe in the equal value of human lives. Therefore they do not value any idea above human life, although they kill for the sake of ideas. To be precise, they live on the plane of their idea. They justify it, finally, by incarnating it to the point of death . . . Other men, consumed with the same devouring faith as these, will find their methods sentimental and refuse to admit that any one life is the equivalent of another. They will then put an abstract idea above human life, even if they call it history, to which they themselves have submitted in advance and to which they will decide, quite arbitrarily, to submit everyone else as well. The problem of rebellion will no longer be resolved by arithmetic, but by estimating probabilities. Confronted with the possibility that the idea may be realized in the future, human life can be everything or nothing. The greater the faith that the estimate places in this final realization, the less the value of human life. At the ultimate limit, it is no longer worth anything at all."

Needless to say, in 1949 the hour of other men has already struck, immediately after that of the Kaliayevs; Stepan Fyedorov had lost on the stage but he had long ago won in the pages of history. Rebellion, now become Revolution, had only one care, care for efficiency. Far away, and obsolete and "petty bourgeois," were the scruples of the terrorist Savinkov when he refused to take part in an attack on Admiral Dubassov in the Petersburg-Moscow express because "the explosion would kill strangers," or the scruples of his friend Voinevski who announced that "if Dubassov is accompanied by his wife, I shall not throw the bomb." The Lenin doctrine had recodified what the revolutionary had to do; his life had now taken on a sacred character in accordance with the "calculation of probabilities" which ordered him for instance not to give himself up and to leave hostages to be shot in his stead, firstly because such hostages were not technicians of revolution as important and useful as he was, and secondly because the execution of hostages, i.e., of innocent persons, would rouse the people and be of advantage to the cause. In the 1950's there were many to approve of this reasoning and some even showered high praise on the "courage of not giving yourself up." It could be that these our intellectuals would have gained from having a second look, for revolutionary logic makes faster strides than they do. Soon, having come to the end of the calculation of probabilities, we shall have not only those who sacrifice hostages but those who swing a machine-gun round haphazard. "Go on, shoot, there will always be something left."

"He who wills the end wills the means." Seeing that great axiom of our century rising and growing on the horizon like a huge black sun, Camus rose in indignation in the name of a demand on himself which, by good fortune, is outside the reach of dialectic: "I . . . need honor, because I am not big enough to be able to do without it." Was this so abstract a view, as his opponents claimed? If we are to believe them, we must forget some strange manifestations of reversibility which our times have seen. Donning the uniform of another, the Rebel, like the soldier with nothing but "esprit de corps" left to him, becomes a stereotyped character and Rebellion is quick to raise "the mouthing cohort of little rebels, sure fathers of slave-gangs, who in the end offer themselves on every market place of Europe for any servitude." In short, "there is a type of rebellion within conformity which is as distinct from true rebellion as night is from day."

"They say the end justifies the means. It is possible. But who will justify the end? This is a question which historical thought leaves open, but rebellion answers: the means." Everything, lies, "liquidations," Kafkaesque trials, revolutionary muddle, pushed Camus to rise against the dehumanization of our time. But a greater ambition now occupied him, to draw up a balance sheet of rebellion and, more especially, of its contradictions and errors. This was an immense undertaking calling for the broadest political and literary culture and exceptional gifts of synthesis, as well as total vision of history and the world; it required the author to turn back and take up again "a meditation begun in *The Myth of Sisyphus* on suicide and the notion of the absurd" (J.-C. Brisville). In short, the sum of history and of Camus himself. For, even if "with certain authors their works seem to form a whole with each one receiving light from the others and each of them facing and complementing the others," still there is always one work, privileged

95

and vital, which itself alone serves as the mirror. The mirror of Camus' work, I believe, is this work of incredible brevity and density, light in weight and heavy of substance, which is called *The Rebel*.

The book is essentially a methodical one, and it seems

to us that a method is most necessary for the commentary which we owe it and that the simplest way is to study it chapter by chapter. There will perhaps be protests against the dryness of such a lexicon type summary and its unavoidable omissions. Even in its brief extent it is, however, the only one which will enable us to examine stey by step a work which above all is a progress of thought.

I. *The Rebel*

"What is a rebel? A man who says no, but whose refusal does not imply a renunciation. He is also a man who says yes as soon as he begins to think for himself." The most negative revolt (as, for instance, the revolt of a slave who suddenly rebels against an order from his master) inevitably contains some positive element; if I refuse to perform such and such action which someone wishes to oblige me to perform, it shows that there is in me a vague will to the contrary, that "something exists" in man "with which" man "can identify himself—even if for only a moment." Consequently, "I revolt, therefore I exist." Hundreds of examples, however, teach us that rebellion is born not only of oppression personally undergone but, at least as often, of the sight of oppression of others. The rebelling individual has therefore the power of identifying himself with another. "In the absurdist experience suffering is individual" (Meursault, Martha, Caligula). "But from the moment a movement of rebellion begins, suffering is seen as a collective experience—as the experience of everyone (Rieux, Tarrou, Diego, Kaliayev). Consequently, "I rebel, therefore we exist."

II. *Metaphysical Rebellion*

"Metaphysical rebellion is the means by which a man protests against his condition and against the whole of creation . . . The slave protests against the condition of

97

his state of slavery; the metaphysical rebel protests against the human condition in general. He attacks a shattered world to make it whole. He confronts the injustice at large in the world with his own principles of justice." Thus, first, "the most elementary rebellion, paradoxically, expresses an aspiration to order" and, secondly, addressing a higher power which it thereby draws "into the same humiliating adventure as himself," metaphysical rebellion is not to be mistaken for atheism. "From one angle, it is even identified with the contemporary history of religious sentiment."

Metaphysical rebellion, properly so-called, does not appear in the history of ideas, in coherent shape, before the end of the eighteenth century. Of course it can be traced long before that, if only in the person of the first rebel, Prometheus; like the rebel of our day, Prometheus struggles with death and is at the same time a Messiah and a philanthropist. But the Greeks "who kept things as cool as possible" made him a pardoned hero—the very expression "hero" is a sufficient indication that he is a demigod in simple disagreement with the gods, in short, settling a mere family squabble. The ancients in fact were very far removed from our metaphysical reflections. They may have believed in fate, but they believed first of all in nature, of which they were a part. Revolting against nature meant for them revolting against themselves, which they would have held unthinkable. Only some time after did Epicurus and above all Lucretius give expression to all the ill-ease of the "entrenched camp" in which man has shut himself up, with despair as his companion. By then of course the world had received the entirely new concept of a single, personal God, of One responsible for man and pain.

Seen in this light, we are much more the sons of Cain than sons of Prometheus. With Christianity, an attempt is made to "have the reply ready in advance for all the Cains in the world by putting a milder expression on God's countenance." The result is merely a dualism, on the one side the fearful God of the Old Testament and on the other God made man dying on the cross. However, once Christianity is called in question and the divinity of Christ disputed, "the frustrated Jesus is just one more innocent" and "the gulf dividing the master from the slaves opens up again. In this way the ground is cleared for the great offensive against an inimical heaven."

Camus cuts this offensive into three periods, absolute negation, refusal of salvation, and absolute affirmation, each having its hero (or team leader), namely, de Sade, Ivan Karamazov, and Nietzsche.

The Marquis de Sade, whatever has been said about him, is neither a writer nor a philosopher of the first order. For a long time his only claim to fame rested on his having spent twenty-seven years in prison for crimes which his name alone serves to indicate. This long imprisonment is the whole explanation of his works. They are nothing but a long "cry of nature," the cry of the sexual instinct punished, repressed, and heightened by prison life, denying God and morality and demanding total possession of men and women even unto destruction. "Nature is sex, his logic leads him to a lawless universe where the only master is the inordinate energy of desire." So, absolute freedom, with virtue proscribed. "Freedom is crime or it is not freedom." This necessity of crime, inevitably doomed to be organized, calls for closed places, for "castles with seven-foot walls," in which the new society, "a society founded on desire and crime," will function without friction, under discipline and rules which cannot be other than implacable. So different and opposite to Rousseau and the "virtuous" Republicans of his time, de Sade codifies the natural wickedness of man. It is sheer atheism, "All is permitted" in unsullied form. These convents of debauch and torment, however, where, as master and god,

99

reigns a libertine of genius, lose little time in finding in themselves their own contradiction and in the end are no better than gloomy asceticism and hideous chastity. Towards the end of his life, the old, obese captive who had dreamed of a mechanized world of pleasures, failing which he would want the great and final offense the "universe pulverized," is no more than a poor amateur stroller setting up his boards for the entertainment of fools.

Ivan Karamazov, now, speaks in the name of love. In the name of love he takes the side of men and underlines their innocence. In the name of love he passes judgment on God: "If evil is essential to divine creation, then creation is unacceptable . . . If the suffering of children serves to complete the sum of suffering necessary for the acquisition of truth, I affirm from now onwards that truth is not worth such a price." Ivan pushes this rebellion to its ultimate consequences: "All or Nothing." I will not accept my salvation unless all men are saved; one in hell and I refuse it. But men are in hell (evil, suffering, injustice, children dying), and I turn my face away and cry: "All is permitted." But you cannot live rebellion unless you live it to the end. And what do you find at the end? Evil and death (for you cannot conceive of any morality without immortality) and, of course, crime. And so one of the purest of rebels in the end has only "the tortured face of the rebel plunged in the abyss." Incapable of action and torn between his innocence and the logic of killing, he hates death and marches on to murder. It is a terrifying and irremediable contradiction, and Ivan becomes insane, like de Sade.

"When man submits God to moral judgment, he kills him in his own heart. And then what is the basis of morality? God is denied in the name of justice but can the idea of justice be understood without the idea of God? Have we not arrived at absurdity? It is absurdity that Nietzsche meets face to face. The better to avoid it, he pushes it to extremities: morality is the final aspect of God

100

which must be destroyed before the period of reconstruction begins. Then God no longer exists and no longer guarantees our existence; man, in order to exist, must decide to act."

When Nietzsche comes on the scene, God is already dead. Stirner has laid the foundations of nihilism. Nietzsche's first step therefore is to agree to atheism together with all its consequences, a world without purpose, the rejection of Christian morality based on judgment and replacing the man of flesh and blood by a "reflection man," the rejection likewise of socialistic and egalitarian doctrines which are mere continuations of Christianity, and finally the transformation of "passive nihilism" into "active nihilism." How is this done? Certainly not through total freedom. On the contrary, "from the moment that man" no longer "believes in God, he becomes responsible for everything alive, for everything that, born of suffering, is condemned to suffer from life." Then, is all permitted? No, for if nothing is true, nothing is permitted. We must "make of God's death a great renunciation and a perpetual victory over ourselves." The answer lies in the risk: "Damocles never danced better than under the sword." It lies also in heroism, that whole-hearted and exalted attachment to the world, to fatality. Nietzsche will have no salvation; the joy of change is the joy of sinking into final destruction. A God, in truth, there is; it is the world. He who wishes to share in divinity has only to say yes to that world. Accept anything, and you reign over everything. "To say yes to the world, to reproduce it, is simultaneously to recreate the world and oneself, to become the great artist, the creator. Nietzsche's message is summed up in the word 'creation,' with the ambiguous meaning it has assumed. The transvaluation of values consists only in replacing critical values by creative values; by respect and admiration for what exists." In this way, says Camus, *The Will to Power* ends, like the *Pensées* of Pascal, in a wager. But it is a wager which Nietzsche himself was not to make, for "the name of Dionysos only immortalized the notes to Ariadne which he wrote when he was mad." Yes, yes, having reached the end of his logic, Nietzsche went mad, like de Sade, like Ivan.

De Sade and Ivan and Nietzsche, here you have three heroes blessed with a numerous progeny; and here is the beginning of the transformation of rebellion.

With de Sade, it was a simple matter. Our inventor of castles of vice dreamed of a "dehumanization coldly planned by the intelligence." He and his ideas were indeed followed, save on one point: conceiving of crime only in liberty of morals, he has been succeeded by those who legalized it and arch-legalized it. "Crime, which he wanted to be the exotic and delicious fruit of unbridled vice, is today no more than the dismal habit of a police-controlled morality. Such are the surprises of literature." Coming to Ivan Karamazov, it is not his being torn between this and that which we retain, but the vision which today has come to pass of the Grand Inquisitor refusing the bread of heaven together with liberty and offering the bread of earth without liberty. "From Paul to Stalin, the popes who have chosen Caesar have prepared the way for Caesars who quickly learn to despise popes." As for Nietzsche, who considered evil as a means of excelling, as a consent of the soul to what it cannot avoid, "a race of vulgar overlords, with a blundering desire for power," have made him a teacher of lies, violence, and fanaticism. Can we quite clear him of such a parody? No, indeed, and although he has nothing in common with Hitler, he had nonetheless written: "When the ends are great, mankind takes another measure and no longer judges crime as such, even though it use the most horrifying of means." "He died in 1900," Camus added, "at the beginning of the century in which that statement was to become fatal."

102

Whatever the gross misinterpretations inflicted by politics as they developed on the message of these three men, it remains a fact that, in the mind of the rebels who followed them, Ivan's rejection of God: "even if you exist I reject you" has turned into: "you do not deserve to exist," and then into: "you do not exist." With God dead, men are still there, and there is history to understand and make. Before proceeding to analyze this history, Camus "fixes" it in a further definition of the Rebel. The first version was: "I revolt, therefore I exist." Almost at once, after rapid considerations, it became: "I rebel, therefore we exist." And now the final form: and "we are not alone." From this starting point, "man, on an earth which he knows is henceforth solitary, is going to add, to irrational crimes, the crimes of reason that are bent on the domination of man."

III. *The Historical Rebellion*

The difference between rebellion and revolution and the passage from one to the other are the subject matter of this long chapter which takes up almost half the book. The underlying date is 1793; more exactly, the 21st of January 1793, the day rebellion became revolution, when it sent God to the scaffold in the person of his representative on earth, the king.

It was the philosophers and, curiously enough, Rousseau and his *Social Contract* who sent Louis XVI to the guillotine. Until then, rebellion (the heresies, the Reformation) had taken root only in beliefs which were themselves not denied. Spartacus himself, when he raised his gladiators against Rome, had not questioned the city's gods. The *Social Contract* changes everything. "Until Rousseau's time, God created kings who, in their turn, created peoples." From now on, "peoples create themselves." On that 21st of January, Saint-Just, a disciple of

Rousseau, took the sacral content out of history when he killed the king. But, one religion being dead, another succeeds it forthwith, and this was the religion of reason identified with virtue. "Our aim is to create an order of things such that a movement, for all, towards the good shall come into being." Hardly had Saint-Just uttered these words when the unique and necessary means of putting them into effect flashed upon him. The man who wanted a form of justice "which sought not to find a prisoner guilty but to find him weak"—a formula which, we may suspect, met with Camus' admiration—turns at once to the Terror. The good demands heads; virtue cannot have living enemies. Saint-Just at any rate appreciated the enormous contradiction between the end and the means (as is proven by his silence when his own time to die came). The decisive step, however, had been taken. "The Jacobins reinforced the eternal moral principles" and "prepared the way for the two contemporary forms of nihilism: individual nihilism and state nihilism." Reason marches forth, with no more reference to any god, only to its own success. The reign of history opens. And "none can reign in innocence."

"Justice, reason, truth still shone in the Jacobin heaven; performing the function of fixed stars which could, at least, serve as guides." From the nineteenth century, a new notion comes to the front: "Man has not been endowed with a definitive human nature . . . he is not a finished creation but an experiment of which he can be partly a creator." We see that Hegel is now on the stage. Hegel supplies new foundations for the hope of rebellion. He identifies reality with the rational; he enthrones a history without transcendency which takes the shape of a perpetual conflict, which means in practice the struggle of wills to power: "Become what you so far are not." All morality is consequently provisional. Hegel "definitely" destroys "all vertical transcendence—particularly the

104

transcendence of principles. There is no doubt that he restores the immanence of the spirit to the evolution of the world. But this immanence is not precisely defined and has nothing in common with the pantheism of the ancients. The spirit is and is not part of the world: it creates itself and will finally prevail. Thus the emphasis is placed on the end of history. Until then there is no suitable criterion on which to base a judgment of value. One must act and live in terms of the future."

What Hegel destroys is not only transcendency. Coming after the king-killers, this god-killer teaches us that the world is without innocence, being bereft of the spirit. From now until history ends, every human act will therefore be a guilty one. "Innocence is only in the absence of doing, as in the existence of a stone and not even that of a child." "Then how can one live, how endure life when friendship is reserved for the end of time? The only escape is to create order with the use of weapons. Kill or enslave," and the two wings of this alternative the heirs of Hegel will share out as the succeeding century rolls on. The first—kill—gives us the nineteenth-century nihilists and terrorists who resolve the problem of master and slave through philosophical suicide or through sacrifice; the second—enslave—brings forth in the twentieth century a new race of men who proclaim that the slave reaches freedom only in becoming the master in his turn. "Why has the revolutionary movement identified itself with materialism rather than with idealism? Because to conquer God, to make him a slave, amounts to abolishing the transcendence which kept the former masters in power and to preparing, with the ascension of the new tyrants, the advent of the man-king. When poverty is abolished, when historic contradictions are resolved, the real god, the human god, will be the state . . . Cynicism, the deification of history and of matter, individual terror and state crime, these are the inordinate consequences which will

105

now spring, armed to the teeth, from the equivocal conception of a world which entrusts to history alone the task of producing both values and truth."

Individual terrorism, then, first. Kaliayev and his friends, each a new Saint-Just—in the sense that they pay with their lives for the lives they have taken in the name of the ideal—aim at "re-creating a community founded on love and justice, and thus to resume a mission which the Church has betrayed." We have seen what their attitude in rebellion is and how it vindicates them, but now we see the sectarianism of Pisarev, the cynicism of Nechayev, and the double game of Bakunin putting a military cast on the same rebellion in the legitimacy of means. Gradually there comes to the front a doctrine which the sinister clown Shigalev defines in *The Possessed* with the words: "I started from unlimited liberty and have arrived at unlimited despotism," and we have despotism within the sect (and any who are not "on the line" are liquidated), followed by state despotism (as soon as the sect attains power and the guilt of its members is officially broadened into the guilt of everyone).

And, now, state terrorism. For Camus this falls into two categories, according as it involves irrational or rational terror. What distinguishes the first group (Hitler, Mussolini, and Fascism in general) from the second is the lack, despite all appearances, of universal ambition, and the reduction to sheer biological dynamism. "Growth and change," says Junger, "is better than living"; and to quote Rosenberg: " . . . the style in a column on the march! it matters little towards what destination and for what purpose the column is on the march." Seven million Jews murdered, seven million Europeans deported or killed, ten million war casualties line the route of that column led by a "booted and spurred Jehovah" for whom men were "planetary bacilli." And yet, we may venture to say, it could not go far. "Germany collapsed as a result of

106

having engaged in a struggle for empire with the concepts of provincial politics" which could only lead Nazism to suicide. "Hitler is example, perhaps unique in history, of a tyrant who has left absolutely no trace of his activities." Had the German army occupied Moscow, we can be pretty certain that Communism would have contrived to use Hitlerism for its own ends, for it possesses, and possesses fully, the notion of the terrestrial paradise, and that is "its strength, its deliberate significance, and its importance in our history."

Marx, in the words of Camus, is "simultaneously a bourgeois and a revolutionary prophet." And, first of all, an heir to Christianity. It was Christianity, was it not, which smoothed the way before him when it divorced man from nature and taught him that the world is only the sign of a promise which will raise him above himself while engulfing him. Marx follows Christianity in seeing nature as mere scenery backing a stage on which non-consenting man moves towards an ultimate end; but, since he denies Christianity, he in fact revives the Judaic message of deified man taking the place of God without mediator or earthly symbol. What are we to make of this messianism? At bottom, it is essentially bourgeois, is it not? For it has its foundations in the scientistic beliefs of the nineteenth century. It is bourgeois and even conservative. The dogma of scientific progress, a "draft drawn on confidence in the future," and a source of rhetorical optimism, "allows the master to have a clear conscience. The slave and those whose present life is miserable and who can find no consolation in the heavens, are assured that at least the future belongs to them. The future is the only kind of property that the masters willingly concede to the slaves." However, the Marxist prophecy is also revolutionary, being linked to political economy, that creator of antagonisms. Hegel maintained that history is both matter and spirit. Marx will not have spirit as an ultimate substance and puts forward his historical materialism. For Marx, man is merely history and, in particular, the history of the means of production. This is putting man entirely inside a framework of social relationships. "There is no such thing as a solitary man" (which was the prime discovery of the nineteenth century) now becomes "You cannot have a man who is not created by social conditions and is not author and actor on the social plane."

Turning to Marx's "predictions" and "prophecies," Camus shows them as already proven wrong. "Capital and proletariat have both been equally unfaithful to Marx." In fact, the economic crises which were to come thicker and faster have on the contrary become rarer and rarer; share capital has spread wider and wider the money which Marx expected to be in fewer and fewer hands; the complexity of the means of production has led to a proliferation of the small firms which he regarded as doomed, and rural economy has completely broken with him. It is likewise a fact that the proletarian ideal has not broken down national barriers but that national barriers brought the ideal crashing down (1914); that the proletariat has not become a class of paupers, as he foretold, but has seen its standard of living raised; that it has not increased in numbers indefinitely but has moved into other classes (the technicians); that division of labor, which he thought would be avoided, has become inevitable. "Division of labor and private property," he said, "are identical expressions." History has shown the opposite in the rise of the technocrat. This is an event which has equally undermined Marxism's basic postulate, the extinction of class antagonisms through the triumph of the proletariat. "Marx says plainly that there will be no more classes after the revolution than there were social distinctions after 1789. But social distinctions disappeared without classes disappearing, and there is nothing to prove that classes will not give way to some other form of social antagonism." The new social antagonism is a thing we of today are well acquainted with; it is oppression, no longer through arms or money, but through bureaucracy. In short, the working of the very economic forces which Marx so much admired has brought the proletariat to abandon the historic mission he laid on its shoulders and socialism has seen itself obliged to become "authoritarian" and transfer the mission to the doctrinaires, which is the same thing as denying it.

Tragedy follows forthwith. "An end that has need of unjust means is not a just end," says Marx, whose ethical exigencies and talent as a debunker of capitalist society met with praise from Camus; he notes with particular interest in this connection that Marx betrays his preference for speaking of what he knows best in calling his book not *Revolution,* as would be expected, but *Capital.* It did not take long before the rightness of the means was disregarded and consideration given only to their effectiveness in securing the just end. We follow Camus as he reviews all of communist history since Lenin in demonstrating this point. Lenin's victory came only thanks to his sharpening of the same weapons capitalism was already using, combined with his respect for capitalist organization: he is known to have said, "[Communist] discipline and organization are being more easily assimilated by the proletariat thanks to the school which the factory provides." Marx rightly decried the accumulation of capital through which capitalism became more and more oppressive, but, no sooner in power, the revolution, pressing on in its turn with industrialization, realized that accumulation of capital was a matter of technical considerations and not of capitalism. Power had to come first and questions of justice left till later. "Where we once had unearned income we now have the labor of man, and the uninterrupted development of production has not ruined the capitalist regime to the benefit of the revolution. It has equally been the ruin of both bourgeois and revolutionary society to the benefit of an idol, a Gorgon's head, contorted by dreams of unbridled power.''

Marxism, ''not scientific but at best with scientific prejudices,'' sees an end to history which is, after all, very debatable. The achievement of this *"petitio principii"* laid down in ''the language of an Encyclical letter,'' and contradicted by the constant putting-off further and further of the proletarian paradise (now a mere article of faith), leads, it is true, to a kingdom . . . but it is the ''kingdom of ends.'' Quite logically, therefore, Lenin takes the decisive step and sets up a military empire. Liberty must be destroyed if the conquest of liberty is to be achieved. From now on, ''the way to unity,'' the goal of the passionate quest of the rebels of last century, ''passes through totality,'' its opposite. History, it goes without saying, has no love lost for the forces of the past; and Engels said, ''The next world war will wipe off the face of the earth not only reactionary classes and dynasties but reactionary peoples wholesale''; but the forces of the past did at least bequeath their strategy to the new revolutionaries. Autocracy had found its protection in its police forces, and Lenin would now found his revolution on a ''professional army'' of policemen, secret agents, and ''realist monks.'' From this time on, ''the proletariat no longer has a mission. It is only one powerful means, among others, in the hands of the revolutionary ascetics.''

Lenin, of course, a ''passionate lover of justice,'' envisaged these means only for the sake of the end to be attained, the withering away of the state. But quite apart from his admission that he did not know how fast things would proceed towards that higher phase of communism, it is clear to us today that his doctrine is belied by the opposite trend, for the state has become stronger and more coercive. And that is not all. Founded on a doctrine of history, it has now set up the trial as a per-

110

manent feature. Any coherence between past and future which is not purely economic presupposes a constant of human nature which the Marxist church will not tolerate and it consequently condemns and persecutes all intrusions of the irrational, all manifestations of art and civilization which are not subservient to history, all the "heretical geniuses" (Freud) outside the reach of the law. In the new empire, dialogue had become impossible and is replaced by the monologue of propaganda (a monologue of which Camus says, referring to surrealist converts to Marxism, that it is a sinister improvement on whatever they thought up in their earlier days). Even your refusal of the empire through death is not allowed; you "disappear" or you plead guilty before being put to death before the eyes of history. And even living in the faith is not enough; you may be objectively guilty. The church, or even the head of the church acting on his sole discretion, will decide it. The future will make the necessary rectifications as need be, "the matter will be settled later when there is no longer either victim or hangman. Consummating its history in this manner, the revolution is not content with destroying all rebellion. It insists on holding every man, even the most servile, responsible for the fact that rebellion ever existed and still exists under the sun. In the universe of the trial, conquered and completed at last, a guilty race will shuffle relentlessly towards an impossible innocence, under the grim regard of the Grand Inquisitor." And so the great contradiction is finally established and triumphant. For "the ultimate contradiction of the greatest revolution that history ever knew does not, after all, lie entirely in the fact that it lays claim to justice despite an uninterrupted procession of violence and injustice. The tragedy of this revolution is the tragedy of nihilism—it confounds itself with the drama of contemporary intelligence which, while claiming to be universal, is responsible only for a series of mutilations to men's

111

minds. Totality is not unity. The state of siege, even when it is extended to the very boundaries of the earth, is not reconciliation.''

"And here we find the end of Prometheus's astonishing journey. Shouting aloud his hatred of the gods and his love of men, he turns from Zeus in contempt and comes to the mortals to lead them to the assault of heaven. But men are weak or lacking in courage, and they have to be organized. They love and seek joy and immediate pleasures; they have to be taught to refuse, for their betterment, the nectar of each day. So, Prometheus in his turn becomes a teacher, first to teach and then to command. His endeavors have to go on and on, and become exhausting. Men doubt of reaching the City of the Sun and even whether that city exists. They have to be saved from themselves. The hero tells them that he knows the city, he is the only one to know it; the doubters will be flung out into the desert and nailed to a rock, fodder for birds of prey. The others will march on in darkness behind a master plunged in lonely thought. In his solitude, Prometheus is now God, reigning over the solitude of men, but, of what Zeus has, he has gained only loneliness and cruelty. He is no longer Prometheus; he is Caesar. The true and eternal Prometheus is now seen with the features of one of his victims. That same cry which came from the very depths of the ages still rings in the depths of the desert of Scythia.''

IV. Rebellion and Art—The Thought of Noon

SINCE the revolution turns against the rebel and the rebel against the revolution, the definition previously made must be sharpened and refined. "I rebel," therefore I exist, "therefore we exist, and we are alone," is no longer acceptable except in a clearer version: "Rebellion at grips with history adds that instead of killing and dying in order to produce the being that we are not, we have to live and let live in order to create what we are."

Note: "we are" and not "we shall be"; art will illustrate this decisive choice of Camus. It is not without significance that all reformers from Plato to Nietzsche and Marx have mistrusted art, and yet it is inseparable from rebellion since it also aspires to reshape the world. What, in their view then, is its crime? "Ignoring reality"? But the example of the painters (Delacroix and Van Gogh) and of the novelists (Mme. La Fayette and Proust) shows us that art may well question reality but does not ignore it; on the contrary, it exalts that part of it which is beauty, a present, tangible transcendency; it marries nature and history and thereby "realizes, without apparent effort, the reconciliation of the unique with the universal of which Hegel dreamed." Of course this is true on the condition that art avoids two pitfalls, pure formalism and unalloyed realism. But it is clear to all that these two pitfalls are equally two illusions, even impossibilities. Pure formalism, which is art without justice leads to nihilism, and complete realism (or "Socialist realism") soon becomes conscious of its limits (one hundred percent realism is impossible—the only totally realist artist would be God) and slumps into propaganda. What, then, is art? It is a creation and thus the partner of rebellion. "In art, rebellion is consummated and perpetuated in the act of real creation, not in criticism or commentary. Revolution, in its turn, can affirm itself only in a civilization, not in terror or tyranny. The two questions posed by our times to a society caught in a dilemma—Is creation possible? Is the revolution possible?—are in reality only one question which concerns the renaissance of civilization."

What does this civilization rest on? On moderation. For "there does exist for man a way of acting and thinking which is possible on the level of moderation to which he belongs," while "every undertaking which is more ambi-

113

tious than this proves to be contradictory"; and, for that matter, science itself confirms that the world "has no definable reality except on the scale of medium magnitudes such as ours are." Is such moderation an evidence of mediocrity? In no way. On the contrary, it is a tension of the emotions maintained by a constant and heroic effort of the spirit. If rebellion can lay the foundations of a philosophy, let it then be a philosophy of limits, "force and not violence"; let it establish calculated responsibility, calculated guilt, calculated risk, to face all the delusory absolutes of dogma and messianism. "On our way to find and master being, we must start from that small part of being which we find in ourselves" and not deny it to the benefit of an imaginary being. "Learn to live and to die, and in order to be a man, to refuse to be a god": this is the ultimate lesson of wisdom which *The Rebel* sets before us. Then, beyond the nihilism of injustice, of tyranny, and of terror, we shall rediscover love, we shall be again in accord with the world. "In this noon of thought, the rebel thus disclaims divinity in order to share in the struggles and destiny of all men. We shall choose Ithaca, the faithful land, frugal and audacious thought, lucid action, the generosity of the man who understands . . . Our brothers are breathing under the same sky; justice is a living thing."

The appearance of *The Rebel* was the signal for more than one polemical campaign, but the one waged by *Temps Modernes,* a periodical of Sartre, was the hardest to bear for those who were accustomed to link Sartre and Camus in the same affectionate esteem. Here we have two masters of contemporary thought each with his way clear before him, and I can see no other critic whose hostility does not bear out and support one of the themes of the book: "A revolution which is divorced from honor betrays its origins, which have their roots in the sphere of honor."

On the 17th of October 1957, the Swedish Academy awarded the Nobel Prize of Literature "to the French

Receiving the Nobel Prize, 1957.

With Francine at the awards ceremony. The King of Sweden applauds him.

writer Albert Camus" for his works "throwing light on the problems which today face the consciences of men." The news created a sensation in literary circles. Camus at 44 was receiving a reward which only two living French writers, Roger Martin du Gard and François Mauriac, then shared. He was applauded and he was sneered at. In the award made to him I believe Camus saw first and foremost the opportunity of reaffirming his writer's vocation, which he did on the 10th of December in Stockholm in the customary speech of acceptance and on the 14th in the University of Uppsala in a lecture entitled *The Artist and His Times.*

"Is art a deceptive luxury?" Yes, if it descends to the level of sheer entertainment for a commercial society. The artist worthy of the name, however, will not be content with the role of amuser, his apparent liberty masking a state of oppression, and with saying amen to the unhappiness of mankind. There will then be a great temptation either to take refuge in malediction or to betray the reality which one is seeking to improve by deforming it into a political doctrine. Finding the just measure for the reality content within a work of art is therefore the artist's major problem. For "to me art is not a solitary delight. It is a means of stirring the greatest number of men by providing them with a privileged image of our common joys and woes." The real aim of art is not to be judge or legislator, but to understand. "Who, after that, would expect of him ready-made solutions and fine moral codes? Truth is mysterious, elusive, ever to be won anew. Liberty is dangerous, as hard to live with as it is exciting" (but the very danger disciplines art and makes it classical). Truth and liberty, then, are the two ends towards which we must march resolutely and with clear insight into our failings. Where is the writer who would dare to stand as a preacher of virtue? "As for me, I must say once more that I am far from all that. I have never been able to forget the delight in life, the freedom in which I grew up. But although that nostalgia explains many of my mistakes and shortcomings, it doubtless helped me to understand my calling, and it still helps me to stand implicitly beside all those strong men who, throughout the world, endure the life that has been made for them only because they remember or fleetingly re-experience free moments of happiness."

Fame had come. Camus was now a celebrated author and, you could even believe, a happy one. But let us make no mistake about it. In 1957, applauded and fêted as he was, admired or hated, Camus was already, as he would remain until the day he died, a solitary man eagerly seeking his kingdom. Through the flood of events on all sides he advances, as he had foretold, "ill at ease, guilelessly walking a tightrope, not sure whether he will reach the other side." This is a man in exile.

EXILE AND THE KINGDOM

Madagascar, Tunisia, Morocco, Indochina: only just freed
herself, France is brought before the tribunal of liberty.
When, however, on the 1st of November 1954, Algeria
rises in its turn, Camus sees the importance of what is
happening. It is his homeland, his native country which is
slipping from under his feet.

Let us look at what he had written in 1939 in his *Kabylia
Inquiry:* "Looking at this immense landscape, I could
understand what the bond was uniting these men [the
Arabs] with each other and what it was that bound them to
their soil. How, then, could I fail to understand their wish
to look after their own lives and affairs and their deep
desire finally to become what they are to a profound
degree, conscious and courageous men—from whom we
can, without being ashamed, take lessons in nobility and
justice?" At the time of the troubles in Guelma and Sétif,
in May 1945, Camus takes up his pen again, to write in
Combat: "On the political plane, I wish to say once more
that the Arab people exists . . . " He denounces once
more the two evils afflicting Algeria: want and injustice.
He traces the history of the situation, reproves the colon-
ists for their eternal deafness to native claims and their
sabotage of timid reforms decided on in Paris; he speaks of
the bitterness of the Arabs and their refusal of the assimilation which they would have accepted twenty years earlier

and now regard only as a new "tool for colonializing"; finally, rejecting the traditional picture of the rebel, he gives the French public an honest portrait of the leader of the Manifest Party, Ferhat Abbas, an Algerian of full French background, a devotee of Pascal, a mind "both logical and enthusiastic." And he ends with these words: "we must at all costs bring peace to these peoples torn and tormented by sufferings that have gone on too long . . . The infinite power of justice, and that alone, will help us to reconquer Algeria and its inhabitants."

Words gone with the wind. War breaks out and splits France in two, as did the Dreyfus Affair. Those of the Right see no problem: Algeria is a French province, so there cannot be any war but only a separatist revolt and treason. But what about reforms? To begin with, the Right wants only the status quo: crush the rebels and start again were you left off. Then, on the 13th of May 1958, the Right is converted to integration, which logically ought to have been its position from the outset. The Arab is declared a Frenchman through and through: his Algerian nationality is stifled in an embrace for love of national union.

For the Left, on the other hand, Algerian nationality is a real thing, even if born only of revolt. The war against Algeria is therefore in truth a foreign war and not a police operation. It is, moreover, an attack on the liberty of a people and therefore unjust and criminal. There must be negotiations with the F.L.N. (National Liberation Front). The Algerian republic must be recognized, for what is the difference between the Algerians and what they fight for and the struggle of the French Resistance during the late war? There are some who will even push this reasoning to its logical conclusion and give aid to the F.L.N.—"liberty is one and indivisible."

There was the choice, and each camp, of course, counted on Camus' adherence. They did not know him

118

well, for he could belong neither to one party nor the other.

What was behind Camus' attitude during the war in Algeria? The very foundations of his being and his work. He was an Algerian and believed in man and earth in harmony, in any solution which did not separate man from nature. He called for moderation, for middle-of-the-road solutions for problems of mankind that were neither great nor small. He enhances the differences in order to attain unity. Before declaring him a "traitor" to this or that undertaking dictated form outside, one should consider whether he was a traitor to the prime undertaking of all, the undertaking you assume towards yourself. This he was not.

What was at stake was not a choice between mother and justice, for the simple reason that mother and justice are one and the same thing. If the fruits of plenty are to spring forth from the country of your roots there must be justice on that native soil. Can we say that Algeria had two kinds of children? Politically, yes, but nationally, no. It is not hard for Camus to show that he is as Algerian as the Arabs. True, the French of Algeria have committed the crime of uprooting the Arabs from their own soil. Are they then to be uprooted in their turn? Or is a reconciliation to be sought, it being fully understood that reconciliation will not come except under certain precisely defined conditions?

If Arab demands were responsible for the war, it was because, despite their solid basis of right, they were equivocal. Their legitimate bases are four: "colonialism and its abuses which have become institutional; the perennial lie of assimilation ever proposed and never put into effect; the manifest injustice of land and income distribution; and psychological suffering" from the contemptuous attitude of the colonizer. All this calls for revolt and would be its justification. But Arab demands are also lacking in legitimacy, for national independence in Algeria is "a conception springing wholly from the emotion. There has never yet been an Algerian nation." Today, the Arabs are not alone to form Algeria. "The Algerian French are likewise, and in the strongest meaning of the term, natives." Moreover, what is political independence without economic independence? Eyewash, no more no less, and subjection to some vague Arab empire under Nasser. Therefore, says Camus, Arab demands will in the end lead to the new territory being handed over to totalitarianism.

His analysis can be found in the text of *Algeria 1958,* extracted from the *Algerian Reports (Actuelles III)* which Camus presented as a memorandum "in the shortest possible space and staying as close as possible to the realities of the Algerian situation." It falls into three sections: a listing of the causes of the war, manifestly incomplete; predictions on an independent Algeria which no one, at the present moment, can confirm or invalidate, although we can see even now that they tend to be more than probable; and, lastly, the denial of an Algerian nation. Is Camus then an "ultra," a reactionary? Obviously not, since he hastens in an appended text to put forward a statute for Algeria which rules out any integration of a colonialist stamp and grants the Arabs autonomy and the power to settle by themselves all problems that concern them. Where is the difference? It lies in this, that Arab demands are expressed in terms of nationalism, and Camus is stressing the *patrie.* There is an Arab *patrie* with its rights which must in the end be given satisfaction, but if it lets itself drift into a nationalism, it wipes out the other *patrie,* that of the Algerian French living side by side with the Arab *patrie* and also having its rights. The solution therefore is not to create a new nation but to federate the two patries, not to cleave but to unite; a federal solution, a "middle-of-the-road" solution, respecting Algerian soil and the races mingled on it. It would be wrong, again, to

120

regard this moderation, this middle way, as a sign of mediocrity, and still less as reactionary or worshipping the past. In fact—and it will not be long before it is more clearly perceived—it is nationalism itself which in the twentieth century is reactionary, whatever are the "progressive" allies it occasionally finds. The proof is that these allies have hesitated to support it; the Communists (with the federation of Mohammedan peoples in the U.S.S.R. before their eyes) long regarded Arab nationalism as a bourgeois phenomenon. And, let us make no mistake, despite its popular aspect, that is what it is, like all nationalisms. The future is not with the formation of isolated nations obliged, for their survival, to cast out their foreign elements. It belongs to broad groupings of autonomous regions, the coming together in freedom of all the *patries;* it belongs to a world state made up of independent provinces and not of separate nationalistic states.

What Camus is standing for is a progressive vision of the future, and also a wonderful experiment which, with a minimum of good will, can be made in Algeria, the meeting place of two continents and two races. If you only will it, the old crime of colonialism can bring forth a first pact of fraternity. But war breaks out, in large part due to the political immaturity of the Algerian French, and Camus knows only too well that being evil it can only end in evil. On the outbreak of hostilities, he does the only thing that could be expected of him. He does what is most urgently required. He takes his stand "in the no-man's land between two armies" and proclaims that "war is a deception and that bloodshed, if it sometimes makes history progress, makes it progress towards even greater barbarism and misery." In a message to Aziz Kessous, the Algerian socialist militant, he says: "Hence we are pitted against each other, condemned to inflicting the greatest possible pain on each other, inexpiably. Nevertheless, you and I who are so much alike, having the same background, sharing the same hope, having felt like brothers for so long

121

now, united in our love for our country, we know that we are not enemies and that we could live happily together on this soil that belongs to us."

"We are not enemies," but they are, for war transforms men. On the 22nd of January 1956, no longer able to avert the conflict, he attempts to mitigate its horrors. In the very capital of a country at war, he launches an *Appeal for a Civilian Truce,* entreating the combattants to avoid at least what is irreparable, the slaughter of innocents.

"What do we want? Simply to get the Arab movement and the French authorities, without having to make contact or commit themselves to anything else, to declare simultaneously that for the duration of the fighting the civilian population will on every occasion be respected and protected." Why this initiative? First of all because "no cause justifies the death of the innocent," but also because a civilian truce is the only guarantee of a peace other than one of corpses and ruins. "Reason clearly shows that on this point at least French and Arab solidarity is inevitable, in death as in life, in destruction as in hope. The frightful aspect of that solidarity is apparent in the infernal dialectic that whatever kills one side kills the other too, each blaming the other and justifying his violences by the opponent's violence. The eternal question as to who was

Draft of the appeal for a civilian truce.

first responsible loses all meaning then. And just because they could not manage to live together, two populations, similar and different at the same time but equally worthy of respect, are condemned to die together, with rage in their hearts."

Once more then—and it is the last time—Camus lays stress on the differences there must be: "(As for me, I believe only in differences and not in uniformity. First of all, because differences are the roots without which the tree of liberty, the sap of creation and of civilization, dries up)," as he stand before a dual people who have at last come together, but for the worst, and now have only one *patrie,* war. "I know that the great tragedies of history often fascinate men with their horrible visage. Paralyzed, they cannot make up their minds to do anything but wait. So they wait, and one day the Gorgon devours them." A thankless task it was to stand between the combatants and appeal to reason, but it had to be faced with resolution if they were to deserve one day to live as free men, "in other words as men who refuse either to practice or to suffer terror."

Camus' appeal at Algiers was very near to not being pronounced at all. Up to the last minute political and police pressures almost forbade the meeting at which the most famous Algerian in the world was to speak. Outside, a crowd of Europeans hissed and yelled, "Camus is a traitor! Camus to the gallows!" The thing was decided, war was here and never to be atoned for. Terrifying changes took place; a man became a soldier and the soldier an executioner. With a frenzy bordering on eroticism, each one ransacked the flesh of his fellow man to cause suffering never known before. Bellies were opened and filled with stones, private parts mutilated, children's heads used for footballs, girls deflowered with bottle necks. A victim was especially more exciting if unarmed, a peaceful stroller or a defenseless prisoner. There were many in both camps who had lived up to now in honor, but they shed it without even noticing, as one unthinkingly slips off a coat. There were some who had gone through Gestapo torture chambers precisely because they would not tolerate a people practicing torture; now they were themselves the torturers. Did they reflect on this? You may doubt whether they even thought of it. They were operating in war, in an absolute moral void. They were like the innocents who go into a long dark tunnel, commit the worst of crimes and come out at the other end, innocent again. They would have neither remorse, nor anxieties, nor memories and no one can rightly say whether they should have had any.

What then is man, who does good and evil haphazardly?

The Fall is the only work of Camus that ends on a note of wretched sneering resignation.

More than one commentator has compared *The Fall* with *The Stranger*. In both works, it is true, there is one man, one voice. But between Meursault, the stupendous innocent declared guilty by men, and Clamence, a "judge penitent," a guilty man bringing guilty men to his tribunal, there is as much difference as between noon and midnight, between the high tragedy of a murder in the sun and the petty comedy of daily meanness, between the blazing sky of the Mediterranean and the mists of the Low Countries. Camus takes us again to a northern country, as he does in the story of the Journey to Prague in *Betwixt and Between* or in certain passages of *Cross Purpose,* to give a stifling impression of emptiness. But here there is hardly any homesickness for the south, and one of its few calls, apart from some unforgettable lines on Greece, is the name of the bar, "Mexico City," an Amsterdam dive where, under the expressionless eyes of a gorilla of an owner, Clamence makes what we take, at first, to be a simple confession.

Jean-Baptiste Clamence has not always been the solitary

124

drinker we see, this dubious exile, this shady lawyer counselling pimps and prostitutes, who comes each evening to do business in the café and then goes home to his room in the Jewish quarter, or what was the Jewish quarter, comforted with the warmth that comes from gin, his "sole glimmer in this darkness." A few years before, he was following his calling as a lawyer in Paris brilliantly. He had everything in his favor, eloquence, a fine bearing, a reputation for sterling character. And he was in truth a man of sterling character; under the black gown of the defender of noble causes there beat a heart that was upright and good. A man like this is seen for what he is by little things; Clamence did good every day in secret. "For instance, I loved to help blind people across the street . . . I always enjoyed telling people the way in the street, giving a light, lending a hand with heavy barrows, pushing a stranded car, buying a paper from the Salvation Army girl or flowers from the old-woman pedlar . . . I liked to give alms. A very Christian friend of mine admitted that one's initial feeling on seeing a beggar approach one's house is unpleasant. Well, with me, it was worse: I used to exult." Thus it is clear to us, and it is clear likewise to Clamence himself: this man has "a vocation for the summits." He does not believe in God but he has the conduct of a lay saint, he is honest towards his clients and women, and loyal to his friends, and when they are dying he holds their hands . . . With all this, he was no ascetic, but "made to have a body," and at his ease in it, "freely holding sway bathed in a light as of Eden." In short, "a successful life," with only one misfortune. On evening, on a bridge over the Seine, Clamence, at peace with himself and the rest of men, was lighting "the cigarette of satisfaction," when he heard a laugh behind him: he swung round, and there was nobody there.

Well, well, there was no mystery about it, somewhere in the dark, people were enjoying themselves. But suddenly

125

it was as if another Clamence appears from the shadows, a clear-sighted Clamence, pointing at his double with a sneer.

From this time, Clamence sees himself from the outside. He discovers little by little the other side of his "noble character." By little things, at first. "Why . . . whenever I left a blind man on the pavement to which I had convoyed him, I used to touch my hat to him. Obviously, the hat-touching wasn't intended for him, since he couldn't see it. To whom was it addressed? To the public. After playing my part, I would take my bow. Not bad, eh?" It is not by chance either that Clamence speaks of "parts played." His modesty and goodness have always been put on, feigned, and, worst of all, he was taken in himself. What about his virtues? That accusing laugh tells him they were nothing but eyewash. "I had principles, to be sure, such as that the wife of a friend is sacred. But I simply ceased quite sincerely, a few days before, to feel any friendship for the husband." At bottom, he has never been anything but an actor, and his guideline is: "a double face, a charming Janus, and above it the motto of the house: 'Don't rely on it.'" Does this mean he is a monster? No more and no less than most men. It was merely that his special line as a man of virtue was built, as he now sees quite clearly, on complete indifference. "How can I express it? Everything slid off—yes, just rolled off me . . . In short, I was never concerned with the major problems except in the intervals between my little excesses . . . Fundamentally, nothing mattered. War, suicide, love, poverty got my attention, of course, when circumstances forced me, but a courteous, superficial attention. At times, I would pretend to get excited about some cause foreign to my daily life. But basically I didn't really take part in it except, of course, when my freedom was thwarted."

Are we to believe that just a laugh in his ears and

nothing more has been enough to open his eyes? Well, no, it was only a catalyst. When he goes back through his memories, Clamence finds two or three episodes where his showing was not really very brilliant. There was the day when he had that not very flattering encounter with a woman and that other day when he got his face slapped in the street and the nuisance of it was not that he lost face but that he realized that he had no face to lose. He had been very careful no to brag about such things, even to himself with "that shattering discretion of which I was a master." But something much worse comes sneaking out of one of the back corners of his memory. One night, he was crossing another of the bridges in Paris in one of those gentle drizzles that you get in November and noticed a young woman in black leaning over the parapet. He looked at her and for a moment the back of her neck, "cool and damp," somehow moved him. But he had just come away from one of his mistresses and now he was calm. He goes on. Then the drama breaks. "I had already gone some fifty yards when I heard the sound—which, despite the distance, seemed dreadfully loud in the midnight silence—of a body striking the water. I stopped short but without turning round. Almost at once I heard a cry, repeated several times, which was going downstream; then it abruptly ceased . . . I wanted to run and yet didn't move an inch . . . I told myself I had to be quick and I felt an irresistible weakness steal over me . . . I was still listening as I stood motionless. Then, slowly, in the rain, I went away. I told no one.

"You see, I've heard of a man whose friend had been imprisoned and who slept on the floor of his room every night in order not to enjoy a comfort of which his friend had been deprived. Who, cher Monsieur, will sleep on the floor for us?" It is a question which has a name and this or that religion has given an answer; in another age, Clamence, revealed to himself by the cry of a woman he had allowed to die, would have entered more or less painfully into the communion of the saints. But this is not the age of grace or of saints but the age of the guilty, and we belong to a band of people making its way under the grim looks of the Inquisitors towards "an impossible innocence." Now, what do you do on the morrow of a crime? Clamence takes himself to task, honestly. Guilty of course he is and sees it clearly, but that is not enough, others have to see you guilty and sit in judgment on you. "Yet who can condemn me in this world where there is no judge, where nobody is innocent?" Neither more nor less guilty than all the others, and granted advance absolution by them and by himself, Clamence wakes to a world stripped of transcendency. He cannot and will not believe it at first. Convinced that now at last all will be known and he will be unmasked and jeered at, he attempts to forestall his mockers with deliberate mockery of his own. His deliberate course to evil comes out in debauchery, drinking, public disorder, scurrilous lampoons, such as an "Ode to the Police" and an "Apotheosis of the Guillotine," counter-blasphemies tuned to the spirit of the times (for instance you shout: "My God!" in the middle of an assembly of atheist humanists), but it's all to no purpose; he is not yet very good at it, and the world reacts so lukewarmly anyway. Nothing can wipe out the idea people have of Clamence, and for a good reason, their idea is the mark of their complicity. Clamence now sees that "it is not enough to accuse yourself in order to clear yourself." He gives up his lawyer's rooms and leaves France, to come and take up his last role, in a cheap dive in Amsterdam, the role of judge penitent. For, if "we cannot assert the innocence of anyone, . . . we can state with certainty the guilt of all."

"My fellow man, my likeness"—never before was the expression put into more rigorous practice. In the Mexico City bar, lording it at a table like the "pope" of a huge concentration camp, Clamence takes pains to become the likeness of the other unfortunates. Every evening, on some vague pretext or other, he strikes up a conversation with some lone drinker who has dropped in, gets him into a discussion, and then tells him the whole story of his life. But, note it well, it is not a confession; it is a speech from the public prosecutor. Clamence confesses, but he forces the other to confess as well. He works cleverly and efficiently. "I accuse myself up hill and down dale . . . But let me point out that I don't accuse myself crudely, beating my breast. No, I navigate skillfully, mutiplying distinctions and digressions too—in short I adapt my words to my listener and lead him to go me one better. I mingle what concerns me and what concerns others. I choose the features we have in common, the experiences we have endured together, the failings we share—good form, the man of the moment, in fact, such as reigns in me and in others. With all this I construct a portrait which is the image of everyone and of no one . . . When the portrait is finished, as it is this evening, I show it with great sorrow: 'This alas, is what I am!' The prosecutor's charge is finished. But at the same time the portrait I hold out to my contemporaries becomes a mirror."

What are the fellow's reactions, faced with the mirror? With long accumulated experience, Clamence cuts them off with a movement of the hand. "No excuses ever, for anyone; that's my principle at the outset." No indulgence, but no condemnation either. "With me there is no giving of absolution or blessing. Everything is simply totted up." You've been to confession to Clamence, but you come out neither condemned nor whitewashed but defined and labelled for the category you belong to. "It comes to so much. You are an evil doer, a satyr, a congenital liar, a homosexual, an artist, etc." From this moment, everything runs normally, and all you have to do now is to sign up consciously and conscientiously in the

129

new world, the world of the great Prophecy. "You see in me, *très cher,* an enlightened advocate of slavery. Whether it's philosophy or politics, I'm in favor of any theory which refuses man innocence and any practice which treats him as guilty. When we are all guilty, that will be democracy."

It is democracy, right enough, with an "empty prophet for shabby times," as J. B. Clamence dubs himself, a new John the Baptist going before, a voice crying out in the desert.

However desperate the judge penitent may be, a beam of light remains, the memory of a voyage to Greece, a vision of ineffable purity and fraternity. "Since then, Greece . . . drifts somewhere within me, on the edge of my memory." Beauty of the past in Greece, beauty of the present in Holland (let us not resist the temptation of quoting this in full: "Holland is a dream, Monsieur, a dream of gold and smoke—smokier by day, more gilded by night. And night and day that dream is peopled by Lohengrins like these, dreamily riding their black bicycles with high handle-bars, funeral swans constantly drifting throughout the whole country, around the seas, along the canals . . . the sea, the sea that leads to Cipango and to those islands where men die mad and happy.") Then there are the doves, fluttering in the Dutch sky or floating down as snowflakes light on the sea; Nietzsche, speaking of doves, said that the really great ideas are brought to us on their feet. But Clamence is the prophet of times of servitude and will have nothing of salvation through beauty. Beauty, the feeling for the beautiful and the creation of it, the proof of the greatness of man, Clamence has shut up in a cupboard, yes, a canvas of Van Eyck, *The Just Judges,* stolen and replaced by a copy which the mob of our century cannot tell from the original; Clamence had left it for a while in the care of the gorilla-barman who mauled it about like a sweat-rag, and then took it back to

130

wall it up in a hotel bedroom, where its sole utility now might be one day to get Clamence arrested, "a chance of being sent to prison—an attractive idea in a way." A nice ending, and a logical one, don't you think? "Ah, *mon ami,* do you know what the solitary creature is like as he wanders in big cities?" Away with salvation, away with hope.

"Are we not all alike, constantly talking and to no one, forever up against the same questions although we know the answers in advance? Then tell me, please, what happened to you one night on the quays of the Seine and how you managed never to risk your life. You yourself utter the words that for years have never ceased echoing through my nights and that I shall at last say through your mouth: 'O young woman, throw yourself into the water again so that I may a second time have the chance of saving both of us!' A second time, eh, what a risky suggestion! Just suppose, *cher maître,* that we should be taken literally? We'd have to go through with it. Brr . . . ! The water's so cold! But let's not worry! It's too late now. It'll always be too late. Fortunately."

One feels some hesitation in saying it, and yet . . . Although Camus in a confidential moment had told a friend who had been the original of Clamence, there is no doubt that the character he created reflects the author himself, sometimes as a negative picture, sometimes as a protest against the ideal portrait some had painted of him, the master of thought and teacher of virtue that he was the first to laugh at. *The Fall* is a continuation in novel form of *The Rebel.* It takes us down into the world of the guilty into which history has taken us step by step. Yet, after all, this is a fall which is possible only because man, outside history, has let go of his own will. It was enough, it is still enough, to jump into the water and save the girl. If he will not, it is his nature that is against it. He is capable of imagining salvation but incapable of making the "leap" to

131

attain it, and an original moral defect dooms him to the role of a comedian who merely mimics the good. This is not only the fate of Clamence but the fate of us all, and Camus' fate. True enough, at a certain moment, Camus abandons the character he has created to the logical development of the tale. But there is the character and his make-up, and Camus is in him and to be seen. What we have to see in *The Fall* (and the humorous tone it has must not mislead us) is a meditation of Camus in face of the absolute; we have to see the state of exile, exile in the midst of other men, with grace lacking to be them, to lie on the floor for them, to live and die with them and in them; exile likewise in the man alone, since the ideal side of him stands on a shore from which he can only contemplate it, with his heart sick with longing and help-lessness.

Is there then only exile? Is there not also, somewhere, the kingdom?

In taking these two words as a title, Camus points to the theme of the short stories they cover, the quest for a *raison d'être* or the wondrous finding of it and, by contrast, the horror of sinking into a world of degradation. It is useful to know that *The Fall* was to be published as the first work in this collection. It includes a story which, in many respects, recalls Clamence's experiences. This is *The Renegade*, the story of a young Christian missionary eager for martrydom, who goes to evangelize a village in the desert. He is taken prisoner by the natives who cut his tongue out and oblige him to serve their own cruel god. Forced to kneel before this idol, the priest of Christ ends by worshipping it of his free will. He recognizes the power of evil and cherishes his slave situation, and when a priest of the religion of love finally appears to rescue him, he kills him. Here again, a bitter tale illustrates the chapters of *The Rebel* devoted to acquiescence in servitude, but it is a whipping also for the Christian Church which has come to terms with Caesar, settled down in the order of violence and "crucified Christ upside down" (Nietzsche).

The other stories in *The Exile and the Kingdom* are of a less terrifying tenor. In *The Adulterous Woman*, the unsatisfied wife of a mediocre traveling salesman, stands one night on a terrace overlooking the desert and discovers all the tender beauty of the world; it is a deeply disturbing picture which the author takes away as soon as he gives it to us. In *The Silent Men*, a group of cooperage workers, on the morrow of a strike that has failed, respond with silence to the advances of the boss who yesterday refused a raise in wages; suddenly, the boss's little daughter falls ill with an illness that may be fatal and we see the workmen's worthy silence turned into a cruelty. In *The Growing Stone*, a French engineer in charge of the building of a bridge in Brazil finds himself at a ceremony in the course of which, in pursuance of a vow, a native must carry a huge rock on his shoulders as far as the door of the church. He has taken his strength too much for granted and collapses. The engineer carries the rock for him, but, instead of paying homage with it to the church, he dedicates it to his friend's hovel. For this world, for this world alone.

Let us stop here a moment, to recognize in these stories an essential constant of Camus, love of nature as opposed to submission to religion and morality, salvation through beauty and mother earth. Janine, the "adulterous woman," does not deceive her husband with another man, not the soldier for instance, who looked and looked at her in the bus, but with the "expanse of night" to which she opens her eyes and her body. "Then, with unbearable gentleness, the water of night began to fill Janine, drowned the cold, rose gradually from the hidden core of her being, and overflowed in wave after wave, rising up even to her mouth full of moans. The next moment, the whole sky stretched out over her, fallen on her back on the cold earth." D'Arrast, the engineer in *The Growing Stone*, is

133

under the fascination of the Brazilian forest, and the workman Yvars (in *The Silent Men*) can no longer look at the sea except in softer evening hours, for it reminds him of his youth that has fled and his freedom sacrificed to his working day. These stories, however, have another point in common, the false situation, a sign of exile: Janine obliged to conceal her feelings from her husband, D'Arrast a stranger among the natives, the workmen in the cooperage condemned by the silence they have imposed on themselves never again to be understood or to understand. This is the false situation which the two other stories of *Exile and the Kingdom* bring into the glare of the footlights.

The Guest is set in Algeria, in a village school on the side of a hill. It is winter, there has been snow, and the children have stayed at home. The teacher Daru is alone, but not for long. A gendarme comes, with an Arab with his hands tied and at the end of a rope. He has committed a crime, some dark family business. The gendarme cannot take him to the jail in town, for the village would then be unwatched and he gives the job to Daru. At first Daru refuses, but the gendarme is astonished that a friend can refuse to do such a service. Anyway, it is an order. Left alone with the Arab, Daru takes the ropes off him and gives him something to eat. If the man took off during the night, all would be well, but the Arab also seems to be the prisoner of a false situation and does not make good his escape, and Daru is forced to act. He takes his "guest" outside, to the limit of the plateau and leaves him there. "You can choose, this way is the town and the police, and that way are the nomads and freedom. The Arab sets off for the town and Daru goes back to his school. He has lost the friendship of the gendarme and on the blackboard in the classroom a message awaits him, to this effect: " 'You handed over our brother. You will pay for this.' Daru looked at the sky, the plateau, and, beyond, the invisible lands stretching all the way to the sea. In this vast landscape he had loved so much, he was alone."

The experiences of Daru, we can see, reflect those of Camus during the war in Algeria. *Jonas or The Artist at Work*, for its part, recalls a confidence made to J.-C. Brisville in 1959 when he had inquired about "the earliness of Camus' success" and was told: "It is true that I experienced the servitudes of having a reputation before I had written all my books. The most obvious consequence of this is that I have been obliged, and still am obliged, to struggle against society to find time for my work. I manage, but at a high price." Camus said further in a letter to P. B.: "My work has not freed but enslaved me."

Jonas, the "artist at work," is a painter and a happy one. By extraordinary good luck, he has had an early success, he has commissions, money, and fame, as well as a wise and good wife and three charming children. Success brings friends, friends without number at the door and on the telephone, a flood of visits, lunches, conversations ("Do go on working! Do as if we weren't here"), then of course requests for assistance, raids on his purse, political petitions to sign. Worst of all, disciples, there is a Jonas School. "Jonas's disciples explained to him at length what he had painted, and why." In short, a mob in the house. "Thus the time went by for Jonas, who painted amidst friends and pupils seated on chairs that were now arranged in concentric circles around his easel. Often, in addition, neighbors would appear at the windows across the way and swell his public." You can guess the result; his disciples and admirers, his friends and enemies are driving the gentle Jonas straight into madness. He tries to get away and the walls are in his way. He sets up his easel in the corridor, in the bathroom, in the kitchen, all to no purpose. In desperation, for you have your kingdom where you can, he fixes a sort of shed of planks under the corridor ceiling. Alone at last up there, he paints and

paints. But is he really painting? One morning they have to get him down and put him to bed and call the doctor. The doctor is reassuring: "It's nothing really, he's been doing too much." What do they find in the shed? nothing but an untouched canvas, "a canvas completely blank in the center of which Jonas had merely written in very small letters a word which could be made out, but without any certainty whether it should read solitary or solidary."

Solidarity, stand fast by your fellow men. With the times making greater calls than ever on the intellectuals, Camus had stayed on the job, with *Alger Républicain*, the Resistance, *Combat*, and again, in 1949 and 1950, he was one of those who directed public attention to the fate of the Greek Communists condemned to death, signing two appeals for them. In November 1952, he resigned from UNESCO after Franco Spain had been admitted as a member. On the 17th of June 1953, at a meeting in the Mutualité, he spoke out for the German strikers killed in the riots in East Berlin. In November 1956, after the Hungarian uprising, he called on European writers to take the matter to the United Nations (and that was not all, he gave material support—although nobody knew about it until after he was dead—to the families of Hungarian writers executed or imprisoned). I have no need to recall his attitude to the Pasternak affair, I suppose. On Algeria, it is true, he said nothing more after his *Algerian Reports*, but his friends were well aware that his silence meant neither lack of interest nor inactivity. A year before his death, he was still striving quietly for a fair solution. You could see many an intellectual, famous or unknown, delivering themselves of declarations full of flame and fury, but you would have to look for the Nobel Prize winner in back-street cafés and there you could find him and Arab friends studying a text he had prepared with some hope of peace.

All these endeavors were in vain, for the war was now once and for all sinking into childish pettiness and horror.

You now hear nothing but magic formulas flung across from one camp to the other, as each side excommunicates the enemy. Persuasion has yielded to intimidation and to lies. The day after the reception in Stockholm, Camus found himself obliged to send corrections to jounalists who had once been his friends and were putting it about that he had publicly denied the torturings. In 1957 he collaborated with Koestler on a passionate and reasoned pleading against the death penalty. He believed in going straight to the springs of evil but it only earned him a stream of sarcasm from those who see only effects and never delve into causes.

Needless to say, there were not only attacks. Camus was making readers and friends every day that passed; he would also not have been a real creative artist if he could not have found a response in solitude. When J.-C. Brisville asked him: "What was your first reaction to all these personal attacks?", he said: "First of all, I felt hurt . . . And then I soon rediscovered the notion on which I normally rely whenever things go against me: that this was in the order of things . . . No, everything that happens to me is good, in a sense. Besides, these noisy events are essentially secondary." Camus felt in himself an effervescence, "a superabundance of life-giving and restoring forces," he was conscious of what he humorously called "a rather disturbing vitality," and would not let himself be diverted from his purposes by any contingencies of "a continuing plague epidemic." However, there is no fighter who does not at times want to sit down and get his breath back. "One may long, as I do, for a gentler flame, a respite." This respite "in the very thick of the battle," where is he to find it? Where is the place where he can find it again?

"Thus, though I possess nothing, have given away my fortune, camp by the side of all my houses, I can still be blessed with all the riches when I choose, set sail at every hour . . ." But where to? The world is now that "little-ease" with its inventiveness that so horrified and delighted Clamence; you have to "take on an awkward manner and live on the diagonal. There are no deserts any longer. There are no more islands." You have only towns where life is tighter and tighter and more and more gloomy and man lives under the pitiless eye of man. You are surrounded by misunderstanding and hatred, and false situations paralyze the smallest thing you try to do.

And yet, and yet there is a kingdom. Camus, happy and delighted, is leaving for that kingdom to shut himself up in it for a while.

Clamence had said: "The Sunday games in an overflowing stadium and the theater, which I loved with an unparalleled devotion, are the only places in the world where I feel innocent."

What is the theater? It is a nowhere kingdom with laws, traditions, and internal regulations all the stricter for working in a closed vessel and responsible only to themselves. The outside world stops at the stage door. It is a privileged world that you can hate or ignore; you can laugh at its oddities and extravagances and its supporters take every opportunity. But make no mistake: if the churches and dictators have always been against the theater, it was its innocence that was the thorn in their flesh, and it was also because truth never shines forth more brightly than from the stage with its masks and strange attire. For the theater is illusion and the opposite of falsehood.

But again, this realm of innocence, the theater, is also a realm of justice, as Georges Lerminier subtly reminds us when revealing Camus' major reason for returning to it. It is a closed world where everything is possible, where heart and mind see no justice except in the highest quality of work on the stage, where everything is done in the last resort as the author desires and requires and everything has a meaning. There is also the humble justice of work meeting with the immediate approval of the public. It is easy to understand that everywhere, and even in the smallest village, there are so many who seek in the theater an off-set for the frustration of their lives—in France there are thirty thousand troupes of amateurs.

In Camus' life history, the Algiers troupe *The Team* up to 1953 was good for an anecdote or two. Camus in his youth had amused himself with the affairs of the theater, and this was good; he had staged several plays and acted in them; this was still better. To that at least we owe an unexpected photograph of a celebrated author in the role, a minor role of course, of Olivier le Daim in Théodore de Bainville's play *Gringoire* put on in Algiers in 1935. It was generally agreed that the fact of having dabbled in the dramatic art had been a useful thing for the author of *Caligula*, but that was all. There were some who were better informed, including the actor Négroni and the poetess Blanche Balain, who had been members of *The Team*, and they have told us how great was Camus' talent as an actor and as a producer. In 1944, Sartre had had in mind to give him the part of Garcin in *In Camera*, but in the end the part was given to Michel Vitold.

In 1953, Camus suddenly came back to the theater to work on the stage. It was in connection with the Angers Festival. In the last three or four years, and more exactly since Vilar's triumph at Avignon, such festivals, joining together the prestige of the theater and the joys of the open air, had become the fashion. The city of Angers did not want to be seen lagging behind and had offered the courtyard of its castle to Jean Marchat and Marcel Herrand. Two plays were announced, the *Dévotion à la Croix* of Calderón and *Les Esprits* by Larivey, both adapted by Camus and, to the general surprise, produced by him. It was an eye-opener, for Camus, in one stride, was in the ranks of the best professionals. The critics greeted the achievement with one voice in long accounts of the splendid internal coherence of *La Dévotion* on the castle ramparts, the admirable "production" of the beautiful

Maria Casarès, and the unfailing high quality of the performance.

Let us, however, look at the matter soberly. Camus did not introduce any new style of producing (as Vilar was doing at the same time). He made some mistakes, there were too many non-professional extras and too much natural scenery—for on ancient walls, any actor inevitably tends to look disguised—and the tempo was a little halting. However, these mistakes count for little against what the tight hand of the producer meant for the overall impression given. Camus was an expert at disciplining a company of actors and imposing his will on them. To each of them he spoke the right words to make him enter into his part. He had a feeling for movement, for the value of foreground and background, and for lighting, and he did not shrink from audacities that would make some of the oldest hands shudder. In short, he showed himself to be an undisputed professional and as much at his ease on theater boards as in a printing-shop. There was the same familiarity and harmony between the boss and the workers, and those who know the theater know that it is a harmony not easy to achieve. Actors are big children whom you must alternately wind up and hold down. Above all you must love them, for they live on their nerves and heart strain and are gambling their lives a little every evening. Camus knew how to make himself understood, and his fame had nothing to do with it, for no reputation you bring in from outside will stand up against the familiarity that reigns on the working stage.

I tend to think that if Camus did not come back earlier to the theater it was because of his health. People thought less about his chest trouble when they knew he hadn't died of it. Nonetheless, and in spite of a vitality which a succession of published works had demonstrated, it is probable that it kept him for some time out of a profession that calls for exceptional robustness. From 1953, at all

141

events, Camus was delighted to rediscover the realm of innocence, because he quite rightly considered himself capable of producing his own plays and those of others; because he is fond of working with his hands (the theater is one of the last really manual jobs, a higher form of do-it-yourself); because what he likes is not "sitting on high and having sway over the void" but working in a community; and lastly, and above all, because happiness for him is in the theater, because it is an "original activity."

In October 1956, the curtain went up at the Théâtre des Mathurins on the *Requiem for a Nun* by William Faulkner, adapted and produced by Camus. Note that here again we have a play of Christian inspiration, like *La Dévotion à la Croix*. What Camus mainly had to do with this well-known "novel in dialogue" was to make cuts and dramatize the cues. The theme is one of redemption in the manner of Dostoevsky: the negress Nancy Mannigoe, to save her mistress from vice and perdition, murders a child and is hanged for it. The *Requiem* coming on the heels of *Sanctuary*, the danger was of losing all movement through the long tirades of Temple Drake, the heroine. This danger Camus avoided by taking the play's lack of movement as his basis for action. He had evolved a very simple setting, for quick changes, with the support of a set of black curtains. He demanded of the cast a maximum of inner tension and a minimum of movement. Melodrama was threatening in the wings, but in Camus' hands the play became a tragedy—not stiff and didactic, as it was with Piscator, for instance, when he produced it in Germany, but harsh and full of life. "With two or three exceptions, I think I have seen all Albert Camus' productions," says Vilar. "His work on the *Requiem* filled me with wonderment, and of course for many reasons. But the one that stays with me and is still quite fresh in my memory is the very subtle hand of the producer over the actors. The

Left: Camus at Angers with Morin, the prefect, who the following year was to become Government Delegate in Algeria. Right: directing Catherine Sellers in *The Possessed*.

evening I saw it the play was past its hundredth showing, but there was nothing heavy or tired about it and nothing relaxed."

Requiem for a Nun was a huge success. It ran for two years, so that the playbill finally carried the names of two Nobel Prize winners as authors, Faulkner and Camus. One evening the actor with the part of the Governor fell ill and Camus took over his part. He demanded that no publicity should be given to his take-over, and it is a pity, for Camus was an excellent actor, sparing in gesture and attitudes, with a deep voice of excellent level and tone, and with a tinge of Mediterranean accent.

In 1957, Camus was again at the Angers Festival and produced *Caligula* and a tragi-comedy of Lope de Vega, *Le Chevalier d'Olmedo,* adapted of course by him. We saw *Caligula* and had to receive it with reservations. It was a strange undertaking, it must be admitted, to wish to

143

acclimatize in Angers, in the open air and on the ramparts of a Renaissance castle, that story of noiseless conspiracy under the Caesars. The *Chevalier d'Olmedo,* on the other hand, delighted its audiences. The play tells a very simple, very brief, and very beautiful story: a noble and handsome young man goes to a village festival, meets a girl, falls in love with her, is loved by her; on his way back, another jealous suitor is lying in wait and murders him. It was a day of rapid events which in Camus' hands became a perfect performance. As for *Caligula,* he took it up again the following winter on the cramped stage of the Petit Théâtre de Paris; but what he now had in mind was to bring off his great stage-work, *The Possessed.*

It was a project in fact that had been on his mind since the time of his work with *The Team* in Algiers. One may ask why anyone should want to adapt Dostoevsky's novel for the theater? Does it not suffice unto itself? This was a basic question we had to ask, and we did, but any prejudices we had largely fell to the ground when we saw the play put on at the Théâtre Antoine and could see its unfailing sincerity.

Of course there could be no question of transferring *The Possessed* to the stage in its entirety. The play lasted nearly four hours, with two short intervals which Camus shortly cut down to one, but all the same whole chapters of the novel had to be sacrificed, including all the chapters about the Governor and the ball and the uproar it caused; the part of Lisa Drozdov was cut down and the long story of the life of Stepan Trofimovich Verkhovenski at Elizabeth Prokofievna's was summarized in a few lines spoken by a narrator. There was one passage, the death of Shatov, which might be expected to be uncuttable in respect of stage time and yet in the end was. But with all the rest, Camus gave a lesson of faithfulness to all those making adaptations. The presentation took the form of a series of tableaus linked up by commentaries from the narrator and

144

nostalgic Russian music. It was a great stage venture and a great success.

The success *The Possessed* had in Paris incited a travelling company, the Herbert Company, to take it the following season to the French provinces and other French-speaking countries. The heart groans to think of what this was to lead to.

Vilar was right in considering Camus as a "stage manager" scrupulous to the last detail. For some months Camus had been working on a novel, *The First Man.* When he learned that his show was going on tour, he decided to make some changes in the production. The cast had been partly changed. Pierre Blanchar was still playing Stepan Trofimovich, but Marguerite Cavadaski took over from Tania Balachova, Huguette Forge from Catherine Sellars who had triumphed in *Requiem,* and J.-P. Jorris from Michel Bouquet. For the "narrator" himself another actor had to be found, and for a while Camus quite seriously thought of taking over the role himself. But there was his novel to write. Camus told Count Antonini: "1960 will be the year of my novel. I have the basic plan ready and I have got down to work seriously. It will take a lot of time, but I shall do it." He gave up the idea and engaged André Reybaz.

The writing of *The First Man* was not the only thing which prevented him from going on tour with his play. For some months André Malraux, the new Minister of Culture, had been thinking of giving him a theater in Paris. We might have seen Camus as a theater manager. He would certainly have made of what they gave him a high place of dramatic art. But was that really what he wanted? In that month of September 1959, I went to see him directing a rehearsal of *The Possessed* in a suburban theater, and he told me that what he much preferred to an enclosed theater in the capital was working in the open air. Why was this? "Because the important thing is to make and train actors and for this there is nothing like Festival theater production.'' He was expecting to go back to Angers the following year and also do the same thing in Oran,

Camus and the children at an outdoor rehearsal.

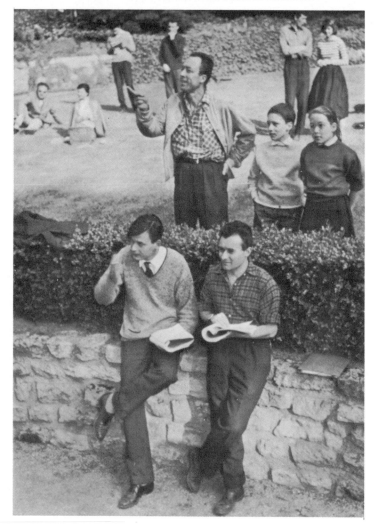

bringing the theater, despite the war, to the wall of Mers el-Kebir. With that he turned again to the rehearsal and I could see him once more in a job he loved, directing his company as if it were an orchestra, with untiring ardor, with his attention to detail, his firmness and his humor.

The premier of *The Possessed* on tour took place at Rheims. Camus was there, left the company for three weeks, and rejoined it at Lausanne. Michel Gallimard went with him. At Lausanne Camus put right the slack bits that had appeared in the performance and left again for Lourmarin to work on his novel, with the idea of not seeing the touring company again until they crossed to North Africa. But he could not refrain from going to find his actors again on two occasions, at Fontainebleau and at Marseilles. Lourmarin is close to Marseilles and it was only a short trip. That evening a photographer of a local paper happened to see Camus among the public in the theater and snapped him. The photograph showed laughing faces all round him (it was the moment of a comic passage on the stage), and Camus' thoughtful face as he watched his people at their work. It was the last photograph to be taken of him.

It was the 4th of January 1960. The Herbert Company had just had three days off in Paris and was going on tour again towards Tourcoing. A friend of Camus was seeing his actress-wife off and asked her "Where is Camus at the moment?" "He's at home, at Lourmarin, at 'The Terraces.'" Methodically, the actress's husband put the name and address on an envelope containing his New Year wishes, and as he posted the letter he mechanically consulted his watch; it was 2:05 p.m. At 3:00 the company's bus set off and later made a halt at Lille. Pierre Blanchar was called to the telephone. "This is Agence France Presse speaking. What do you think of the death of Camus?" The same evening the company was at Tourcoing and "the show had to go on." And Maria Liebadkin,

Maria-the-lame, Maria-the-mad, pointed to a card that had fallen out of the pack and cried: "It is death! I can see death!"

For three days the actors on tour continued to receive letters which Camus had posted at Lourmarin which had followed them as they moved on. And they read: "Bear up. Nice work. I'm not forgetting you. I'm with you all the time."

CAMUS' THOUGHT

The worst that could happen to a writer was also Camus' lot, a rapid blaze of glory while people swarmed around asking questions. "We writers of the twentieth century shall never be alone again." The writer of yesterday had a seat somewhere up in the circle, watching the world show which supplied his themes and subjects; now, the crowds want him down in their midst. They are at him and want his reply on everything. Camus became famous at the height of this public curiosity and trust, at a time when a whole younger generation, waking from a nightmare, was groping for leaders. He was constantly sought after. What a burden this could be he never concealed, but let us put on record that he bore it with dignity that was and is, just as much as his work, the proof of his greatness.

He was not one of those who let themselves be monopolized or who take back something once it has been given. He was simple in manner, attentive, and punctual. For him politeness was the first degree of justice, being the elementary justice you do others. His friendship was demanding, but loyal even in little things, as Péguy has said. I like to remember a man battling with an immense load of work who could always find the time to reply to

148

letters, read beginners' manuscripts, defend the dead and publish their work (Simone Weil). I like also to remember that he always respected those who disagreed with him. His barbs were sometimes super-sharp, but they were never poisoned. Contempt was alien to him.

The only time he was really embarrassed was when people spoke to him about his writings, and then, the mistaken values which people wanted to be compliments would make him withdraw into himself. "No, no, they're mistaken," his inner self objected while outwardly he remained so calm.

"Often, on those theatrical, 'opening nights,' which is the only time I ever meet what is insolently termed *'le tout Paris,'* I have the impression that the audience is going to vanish, that this world, as it stands before me, does not exist. It is the others who seem real to me, the great figures shouting on the stage. If I am to stay, I need to remember that each of these spectators has a rendezvous with himself; that he knows this, and doubtless will be keeping it a few moments from now. Immediately, I see him again as one of by brothers: loneliness joins together those whom society separates. How, knowing this, can we flatter this society, beg for those paltry privileges, agree to congratulate every author on every book, ostentatiously thank the favorable critic, why should we try to seduce our opponents, and, above all, how ought we to greet all those admiring compliments which French society (in the author's presence, at any rate, for once he has left . . .) uses as extensively as Pernod or the sentimental magazines? All this is beyond me, it is true. Perhaps the fault lies with this churlish pride whose powers and range I know so well. But if this were all, if my vanity were the only factor involved, it seems to me that I could enjoy compliments, superficially at least, instead of always being embarrassed by them. No, I am most conscious of the vanity which I share with many members of my profession when I hear certain rather justified criticisms. When I am being complimented, it is not pride which gives me that stupid and clumsy air which I know I have, but (at the same time as that deep indifference which dwells in me like a natural infirmity) a strange feeling which comes over me: 'You're missing the point . . .' Yes, they are missing the point, and that is why a reputation, which is what people call it, is sometimes so hard to bear that we find a malicious pleasure in doing everything necessary to lose it."

As a person, Camus was not easy to get an idea of. What a painter or a sculptor would have made of his face, which was quite different according as you looked at him full-face or in profile, that we shall never know since he never posed except for photographers and that mostly in a pause in the middle of his work, which could then show in many marks of fatigue. Mme. Saint-Clair has given us a pleasing portrait of Camus in her *Galerie Privée*: "thick dark hair, medium nose; long, full cheeks, a slightly ashen complexion bringing out the color, or colors, of his eyes, for they could be yellow or green or grey as you met his watchful direct gaze. His hands are shapely, with expressive movements of astonishing precision accompanying words spoken in a somewhat lifeless voice." But in the end, we have to be content with impressions of his friends, preposterous but not without their grain of truth: "An El Greco!" or "A Humphrey Bogart!" and no one can speak more eloquently than Roger Grenier who says, "If you ask me to talk about him, all I can find to say is things like: 'He always had a raincoat on.' And if you want me to remember his words, what come back to me are jokes in the editorial room."

This is true. Our "intellectual leader" ("As to being an 'intellectual leader,' it simply makes me laugh. To teach, you need to know. To guide other people, you need to know how to guide yourself.") deplored people's inability to see how large was the humor content in his works, and

150

in his life was given to practical jokes. M. Etiemble tells us how he and René Char scared a hotel-keeper by letting him take him for Mad Pierrot, the gangster. M. Emmanuel Roblès has recorded for us his skirmishes with the two cavalry officers put in to censor *Soir Républicain* in 1939. We have already sketched these military men, "severe to excess, finicky, suspicious, and contemptuous." Camus paraded before their eyes thoughts of this kind: "When a man is on horseback, it is always the horse which is the more intelligent of the two. André Maurois." "Men are judged by the use they make of power given them. It is noteworthy that inferior minds always tend to misuse the bits of power which chance or stupidity have given them. *Caligula.*" Another time he ended his article with the sentence: "We must hunt him down, we must fight this scombroid." The faces the censors made! "For a long time they stayed discussing in a low voice. 'Can I be of any assistance to you, gentlemen?' Camus asked with his most conciliatory archbishop's air. No reply, but our censors went off to the Government General. Time passed. We were told that on the hill there was a furious consultation of dictionaries and a hoary professor was brought in. In the end the whole article was suppressed without any explanation given."

And what is his way of working? Standing up, "because I feel the need to exert myself." His method: "notes, scraps of paper, vague musing, and this for years on end. One day, the idea, the conception which causes these scattered fragments to coagulate, comes along. There then begins the long and painful task of setting these into order." Does he talk about a work while it is in preparation? "No." Does he work regularly? "When everything is going well: four or five hours at the start of every day." Does he feel guilty when he puts something off until the next day? "Yes . . . I don't like myself . . . Creation is an intellectual and bodily discipline, a school of energy. I

151

have never achieved anything in anarchy or physical slackness.''

It has been said that Camus invented nothing and that, at bottom, is true. He comes down in a straight line from the Greeks, from Nietzsche, Dostoevsky, Unamuno (and Pascal and Molière, he would add), and from Gide, Malraux, and Montherlant among the moderns, though their influence is much smaller. R.-M. Albérès deserves credit for his penetrating observations: ''Camus is a selective writer who, by temperament, belongs to a line of descent rather than to a period. There are some on whom the hue of the literature of their times does not rub off and Camus is one of these. You could explain the whole of Camus by imagining that the years 1895 to 1933 had not existed. All those who came in the interval between the Nietzschean revolution and the time when the black barrels of rifles were trained on the intellectuals of 1942 are erased: Barrès chained to the rock of traditionalism, Péguy's interminable repetitions, the sophistications of Huxley and Pirandello, the powerful and contradictory Goetheism of Thomas Mann, those who returned to the fold of the faith, surrealism, conversions to revolution . . . '' Shall we say ''erased'' or left behind with a powerful stroke of the wing? In truth there is no landscape that Camus' work ignores but, caring only about the essential ones, it flies on over the others without landing. For a mind contemplating the mighty tides of the Eternal Return, mere ripples of repetition are intolerable, and it is of course on ripples and waves that the literature of a period floats. Camus' eyes were on higher crests.

Note first of all that he never gave himself to literature of pure entertainment. Not that he countenanced that ''hatred of art fostered by the artists themselves'' which brings modern writers to blush for their calling and become the bastards of politics (''in 1957 Racine would apologize for writing ''Bérénice'' instead of fighting in defense of the Edict of Nantes''); but it happened that

152

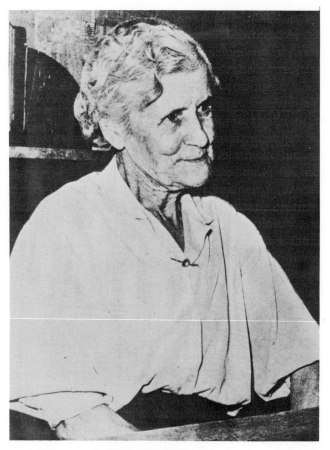

Catherine Sintès Camus.

with the dimensions of his work and the times they were written in, this dilemma never presented itself to him. In 1900 the poet of *Nuptials* would surely have been nothing but a crippled aesthete. A little later, he would have felt authorized, once or twice at least, to tell for the pleasure of telling, like Roger Martin du Gard. But from the 1930's, a towering wave from the great times when art and man were inseparable imposes on the best of their calling both joy and struggle, poetry and action, entertainment and moral lessons. Is this the involvement of literature? It is, but literature must also be totally involved, as it was, for instance, for Sophocles on the morrow of the war for freedom. Each man's failings will be measured by whether he holds the scales level, whether he lets them incline now towards the sun, now towards history. The greatest of them, the one who from all points of view can be called the just, is the author of balanced work in which what was written for his own joy and pleasure is inseparable from the expression of the daily struggle. Joy ends in a precept for conduct and his teaching, even political teaching, bathes in the light of noon.

Such works called for a style spurning the fashion of the day, and first of all a vocabulary that was understandable. Camus leaves to others the philosophical jargon which is to literature what the technocrat is to the workman. He is not a "specialist" writing for the initiated in a language oozing self-satisfied obscurity and, as it comes from certain modern essayists, in a class with that of the précieuses. Here, indeed, Camus has not forgotten the teaching of Molière; he knows that such language is the language of a seriousness that can also be called ponderousness and that in literature as in politics it leads inevitably to distraction, by which we mean forgetting (as M. H. Gignoux says in a study on comedy in the theater) "real life for doctrines, the public weal for the making of plans, and justice for the procedure of the courts." Most of the great crimes of this century owe their birth to seriousness armed with the weapon of technical language; it has filled the prisons, the concentration camps, and the common grave.

So, clarity above all (and even a "return to simplicity." according to Jean Grenier). "A creative epoch in art may be defined as the orderliness of a style brought to bear on the disorder of a time." Camus comes back to the basic words: earth, sea, fraternity, man, honor, liberty, joy, justice, love, and has no fear of using them again and again. (When asked which were his ten preferred words,

154

Camus replied: "the world, pain, earth, mother, men, the desert, honor, poverty, summer, the sea.") We can distinguish two styles of writing in what he wrote, one is sharp and quick, to express facts, indifference, humor, the machinery of history; the other broad and rolling in a great deep swell, for communion, the kneading of times and worlds, and eternity. His sentence has often a hammer-beat and is most frequently brief. Is this a "universal language"? Certainly not, if you are thinking of writers like Céline, obsessed with the wall between literature and the people and "going to the people" with slang and impressionism—however touching such endeavors may be, they are nonetheless contrary to reason. It is not literature that must go to the people but the people to literature. Camus writes with an aristocratic simplicity so as to be understood by those who like reading him. Not all may have the opportunity to read him, but that is the fault of a bourgeois state which keeps the people away from culture. Camus has taken the correct position: the reader will find no mystery in him, but neither will he write down to the reader. No land can call itself properly civilized until all its children, even those on the lowest social level, can reach out to meet him if they wish.

Moreover, what is style? Of course, it is "the man himself," but at the same time the working tool he uses to pierce the dense mystery of life. One of the characteristic features of Camus' style is his standing back from his subject, at its highest a quasi-religious stance in front of a wall considered unscalable, at its lowest self-restraint in face of emotions. At a time when literature wavers and waddles between impersonal commentary and raving con-fession, Camus puts a distance between himself and his subject while putting his whole heart into it. This is what the great artists did; he began as they did, with slow and respectful approach. Before taking up the pen, he looked, looked at his mother and his mother's face, this at the very

155

beginning ("... place in the center of this work the admirable silence of a mother and the effort of a man to rediscover a justice or a love that matches this silence"). Then he touched, touched the sand, the breaking wave, the mastic bushes at Tipasa, women's bodies and that small smooth stone which has the weight of the world. Only then comes what he calls rebellion: for the artist, the attempt to reshape the world "with a slight distortion which is the mark of both art and protest" sets free the desire for creation which stirred within him. "Great style is not a mere formal virtue . . . Great style is invisible stylization or rather stylization incarnate."

From respect through wonder to ambition unsatisfied. The more an artist advances in his art, the more he admires ("that supreme joy of the intelligence which is called admiration"); the more the public believes him intimate with what he expresses and more intimate with each day that passes, the more he knows he is remote from it. "That is why, perhaps, after working and producing for twenty years, I still live with the idea that my work has not even begun," the writer admits. As for the man himself, who prizes above everything "truth and the values of art that reflect it," the time has come to quote some of his most thoughtful words: "If there is a party for people to belong to if they are not certain of being right, I belong to it." For there is a sun-truth, freedom, justice, happiness, obvious and even dazzling, which has proved itself by raising rebellion in the creator, which constantly keeps him company and impregnates him, but remember also that the debate which it launches on earth, in poverty and contradiction, is one which demands the highest degree of modesty. On all sides there is the alternative, this side and that side of a question, exile and the kingdom. Doubt, doubt, and doubt again. Otherwise, your lot will be the worst possible, in politics it will be the certainty that makes a man an unveering prophet, in literature it will be

156

works driving a message home, and thought that is smug, and you will find yourself a bourgeois of the Right or the Left, a traitor to honor in the most elementary fashion. The man must therefore have a style, as the writer must, or rather, the same style will define man and writer. When our author no longer speaks only with his own voice, he leaves his characters such as Meursault or Clamence to speak, or a narrator such as Rieux who puts a distance between his characters and himself. Camus the man, facing his "fellow men," steps back a little, the better to do justice to them. There is no seeking to merge them and himself in totality, but respect for their difference, the condition of the unity he strives for. When he was invited in 1948 to speak at the Dominican convent on boulevard Latour-Maubourg in Paris, Camus made a point of beginning with these words: "I wish to declare also that, not feeling that I possess any absolute truth or any message, I shall never start from the supposition that Christian truth is illusory, but merely from the fact that I could not accept it." This was an attitude that was not always to meet with the like, not from Christians, in particular.

Camus was hardly in his grave when we had the television report of his funeral at Loumarin ending in a close-up of the cross in the cemetery. The cameraman was probably only an unthinking boob who thought it his duty to take that final shot because "it looks good, death and a cross, the good Lord, you see?" Nonetheless that final picture was a glaring insult. It illustrates a naive tendency to regard Camus' work as unfinished, not because of the brutal fact of death supervening, but because "God is not in it." From that point it was only a short step to getting the stray from Christianity back into the fold.

Father Bruckberger admits that "the feelings he expressed were not anti-Christian." Well, of course! Camus was a moralist, like most French writers. Like them, he simply cannot get away from centuries of Christian moral-

157

ity and Christian thought. Being partly tied, in this way, he did not go off to find a god among the Hindus or the Chinese. He inherited Greece and Christianity and accepted it so. On his native soil he built himself a home. He wanted no other and I think he made it clear enough. Did he have temptations? Father Bruckberger says that when leaving priests he had been with he was depressed and disappointed. "It is sad to have to say it, perhaps he had not got what he expected." But what did he expect? That is the whole point.

Camus certainly liked being in the company of clerics, his first reading of *Cross Purpose* was to the monks at St. Maximin. There is a Christian thread running through his works; think of the titles (*The Just, The Fall, Exile and the Kingdom*), the plays he staged (*La Dévotion à la Croix, Requiem for a Nun, The Possessed*), his characters, stage situations, and scenery (Martha and Maria in *Cross Purpose*, the concentric circles of the hell of Amsterdam). How indeed could a writer put behind him words and images heavy with universal significance? How should a man, respectful of the differences between men, not take cognizance of the Church and do this with toleration, interest, and application? Honesty requires us to see two attitudes, Camus in the presence of the Church, and Camus in the presence of God (and even a third, Camus in the presence of Christ). The first does not involve the second any more than the second involves the third; you can be converted to God without being converted to the Church (Simone Weil), just as, without believing in God, you can find in some of his priests fraternal spirits.

Camus knew them as such, and they knew him, we need have no doubt about it, from the endless eager questions he put to them. Most often, when the talk turned on evil, for instance, they were questions which Ivan Karamazov might have asked. Clearly, Camus saw Christians as men very close to himself because they pay due regard to what

158

is sacred and to justice and dignity. On many points they and he were together, they fought side by side, but even in the battle Camus never forgot the underlying ambiguity: the Christian fights less for the world here below than for the world to come. He never forgot that the first act, the crime as he saw it, of Christianity had been to divorce man from nature for the promise or the mirage of that other world. In the fight they fight together, therefore, the Christian allies may have the same arms and the same disciplines but they do not have the same target as he has. They have not the same language either, or rather, theirs is soft and gentle and Camus with good reason reproaches them for the low voice they often use. What name is to be given to fellow fighters who believe that in any event victory is to be won in another place? The answer is to be found in *The Plague* and we come again, precisely, to Father Paneloux. Father Paneloux did give up greeting evil as a vengeance wreaked by God on his creatures, he also took on a most earthly fight at the side of Rieux and Tarrou, and his fight cost him his life, but when they found him one morning, on the floor beside his bed, stiff, and with eyes that said nothing, they put on his card the only appropriate words: "doubtful case."

Camus is intensely interested in the doubtful case and also shocked by it. His demands on Christians are high, because, do as he will, he cannot believe that love can admit evil. Christians (Georges Hourdin) come back with the argument about freedom of choice. Unfortunately, you have the Church to show where that freedom shades into complacency and even complicity—the rebels and even the blasphemers have annexed Christ in the end, but the reason is, is it not, that the Church Triumphant has eagerly replaced him with the God of the Old Testament. However, and it must be said again, if there is an abyss dividing Camus from Christians, it was dug not only by the burners of human flesh called Inquisitors and the cardinals who blessed the bombers and the popes who condemn racism with wry lips in an unintelligible language. Even if Father Paneloux should find a satisfying explanation for the death of children, the abyss would be there all the same. Camus is not of the faith or rather has the faith not to believe. "Thou wouldst not seek me if thou hadst not found me already," and the point is that Camus is not seeking. All that he wrote shows a disinterest in God which any feeling for the sacred neither corrects nor contradicts. A man whose kingdom is entirely of this world holds his peace—and now does so forever—when faced with the futility of what comes after death and even the futility of any explanation of the meaning of life and death.

This the believers have regretted in terms which cannot fail to move us and they go on discussing with him as if they still hoped to convert him beyond the tomb. Camus "spirited away" by death was the inspiration of some admirable pages of Maria Le Hardouin. Marc Bernard, with the absurd as his starting point, attacked what he called his "contradictions," saying, "For me, to say that life is absurd is itself an absurdity. It was all as if he condemned life without hope of appeal—and if life is absurd in its very essence, what is there for us to be indignant about?—and he [Camus] then immediately entrenched himself in a purely human universe, demanding total logic of it. How can one organize order, in any way at all, anywhere at all, if disorder is immanent and unavertable, if it arises from what we are, if it is fatality?" As for William Faulkner, it was of course his Puritanism that was responsible for his forthright words: "He [Camus] said: 'I do not like to believe that death opens up another life. For me, it is a door that closes.' That is what he tried to believe. But he couldn't. Despite himself, like every other artist, he spent his life seeking and requiring of himself the answers that only God knew. Why then did he not give up, if he did not want to believe in God?"

160

Faulkner asked why. The reason is that the quest (not for God, but for the answers) is of the very nature of man. Moreover, Camus is one of the rare writers of our century who knew where to stop in time, he never crossed the forbidden threshold beyond which lucidity is paralyzed.

Claude Vigée in his remarkable study puts his finger on the decisive moment in *The Stranger* when Meursault, on the beach where he is going to kill the Arab, feels the scorching heat of the sun. "I took another step forward, I couldn't stand the scorching heat any longer. I knew it was a fool thing to do, and that I would not get out of the sun by moving a step. But I took that step, just one step, forward." That one step was enough; he had not resisted the sun, or rather he had moved on, and therefore he committed the irreversible action, he entered upon death. "The fate of the Stranger is a warning to the pilgrims to the kingdom." Not so irreversibly as Janine, the adulterous woman, falls back onto the cold earth after being brutally submerged by "the water of night," and Jonas, at the ecstatic glimpse of his star, collapses on the floor of his loft. So many coincidences point to a clear intention: "The mortal danger for Camus, it seems, is in the temptation of making the sacred an active element or of being captured by its power."

It is a long road that leads to this "sacred terror." It starts off most modestly, before a landscape. "If there are landscapes which are states of mind, it must be the most everyday among them," says Camus, and what does that teach us if not moderation? A little later, man will gain "a certain familiarity with the fair countenance of the world." In what way? Not in looking it in the face but rather by taking "a step to the side to behold it in profile." The final fixed stance in the presence of the sacred is only the final stage of the apprenticeship. Let us turn again to Vigée, for it could not be better said than in his words: "Exaltation can be fatal and ecstacy in substantial union can kill human individuality, whereas what Camus wants is only to bring

161

that individuality into accord with the world and let it, in the protection of the retreat which the artist's finely worked figure affords, see only a gleam of that terrible fire which certainly gives us life but can also bring us death.''

There has been talk of Camus' paganism, but this could lead to nothing, apart from his being accused of the sin of literature by those who, in this respect, were much more guilty than he; or else they slyly intimated that the Greeks would sooner or later have brought him to Christianity, forgetting of course that the reflection necessary for that he had already done at considerable length in his young days while studying the Hellenic contribution to the new religion. And indeed, why such ardor to convert him at all costs? Camus was never militant in atheism. I doubt whether any person's faith was ever seriously shaken by what he said. It was not a thing he wanted in any case. But he may have held back on the downward slope to a lazy conversion some minds leaning towards a summary surrender. If this is so, he will have prevented them from finding reassurance, but this only the mediocre could disapprove. Far from depriving them of the power of reflection, he strengthened it in them by showing them the opposite of the easy road, namely, that moderation of which his work gives us the symbol in the bow stretched to its farthest point and yet not launching the shaft. Some will prefer this respectful halt to a blind leap into the unknown or the easy road to the sublime which certain mysticisms offer, not to speak of the "automatic" crosses in Loumarin and elsewhere. And lastly, this reticence in the presence of the sacred puts forward something which is anything but negative, obliging man to contemplate his earthly kingdom and not unload his burden onto a divine baggage man, an external and mysterious will. For the absurd does not destroy man; not in the least "cut-off" but contemplating and following everything around him, he can, even in the midst of disorder, ordain and guide his life adventure and make it worthy of being lived.

Above all else is loyalty. The Camusian man has both feet on the ground; born by chance in a place that chance has chosen, he makes that chance, as he makes his life, a vocation. He has his country, the land of the living, the land of the present. A man can of course live and die in a hotel bedroom, but when the traveler in Prague, alone and uprooted, hears that the man in the next room, the man without a name, has just died, everything suddenly seems sordid and miserable, for the worst deprivation is to be far from your country. "Then I thought desperately of my own town, on the shores of the Mediterranean, of the summer evenings I love so much, so gentle in the green light and full of young and beautiful women. For days now I had not uttered a single word and my heart was bursting with the cries and protests I had held back. I should have wept like a child if anyone had opened his arms to me."

We have seen how Camus' country was threatened by nationalisms which were a hateful caricature of it, and by a debasing uniformitization of the world. A man's country in any case means much more than land itself or the history behind it, it means also the job he does and the way he lives. Camus likes to see a choice made and that choice held to; he has little respect for the atheist who sighs. "My God" or the priest who calls himself an anticlerical. No, loyalty to the daily task and the tools you perform it with is what Camus regards as the highest of man's honors. And here again, as in the political debates about his native country, take care not to attribute his attitude to a reactionary nostalgia.

Camus greatly admired Simone Weil for having gone to live among the workers and for her characterization of their life as an "uprooting." The life of the wage-earner is nothing short of exile. "He may be physically present but morally he has been uprooted and exiled. He is not at home either in the place where he works or where he sleeps, or in the party or the trade union that is supposed to have been made for him, or in places where he has fun,

163

or in intellectual culture." Those famous lines were published nearly two decades ago—we owe it to Camus that they were published at all—and the underground rumblings of the working class only confirm them and bear them out. Neither wage increases nor nationalization of industry, not even the suppression of private property, can make the conditions of the proletariat bearable. "You cannot put an end to the conditions the proletariat lives in with laws and regulations"; what has to be done is "to re-form industrial production and form a culture of the mind so that in them the working man is at home and feels himself at home."

That was Camus' line of thought too. No one has surpassed him in denouncing the horror of work today, but his forceful words did not in any way mean, as some have been too quick to say, that he was turning his back on technical advance. When the workman Yvars cannot look at the sea because it calls up the memory of all the promises of his youth of freedom that have been crushed by the servitude of work, it is not his work (his job as a cooper is one of the last, and that is now dying too, in which the hand sees what it is creating), but the inhuman precariousness of the life of the wage-earner that is at issue. Conversely, if the settler in Algeria has uprooted the Arab out of the soil of his own country, it has been done by keeping mechanical progress away from him, by shutting him out of the century of technical advance. The machine is not the enemy of man; it is only "bad in the way it is now employed." And in any event, in its blind advance, "it imposes its own limits. . . . By dint of . . . excess, a day comes when a machine capable of a hundred operations, operated by one man, creates one sole object. This man, on a different scale, will have partially redis-covered the power of creation which he possessed in the days of the artisan. The anonymous producer then draws nearer to the creator." Science, for its part, appreciates and accepts those limits by virtue of its own origins and its patient and painstaking acquisitions, and if it should forget, if it should put itself at the service of the spirit of power, its punishment is thenceforth to produce only the means of destruction. "But when the limit is reached, then perhaps science will serve individual rebellion. That terrible necessity will mark the decisive turn."

Thus, loyalty to the earth, to work, to the human dimension, and collaboration with material forces. Above the re-established alliance rises the sword of justice, straight and gleaming.

Camus never tires of reminding us that justice is in the first place a personal balance which is constantly threatened, the continued endeavor to see both sides. "He was a born arbiter. He relied only upon himself, not upon any transcendent, and he evades no difficulty. He faces everything, at any moment, with raw moral fact (Georges Hourdin). "I chose justice . . . so that I could remain loyal to the earth. There is no order without justice . . . Justice is both an idea and a warmth of the soul." These last characteristics bring about that "restoration of balance" which is indispensable. For justice must know a limit, and any justice desired in the absolute is only "a convulsion. Let us be wise enough to accept the human side and not make of it that terrifying abstract passion which has mutilated so many men. Destroying freedom for the sake of the reign of justice is like rehabilitating the notion of grace without divine intervention and, in a dizzying reaction, restoring the Mystical Body in the meanest species." And finally, "what is justice without a possibility of happiness?"

For indeed, justice is the first way of approach to happiness, and the second is freedom, which is almost indistinguishable from it, the freedom for which men will die (while for justice they hesitate), which shows that it is the final conquest before happiness, the last key which opens up everything, even friendship: "Friendship is the science of free men." "To sea, to sea!" is therefore a cry to be uttered only after establishing justice, and this only on condition of not making a god of it; then, in freedom, man will also see beauty and will find himself "on the high seas, threatened, at the heart of a royal happiness." This suffices for a man to be able to live, that is to say, to "rush to his doom." It suffices for a man to be able to die reconciled, despite the world and its absurdity, and in possession of the ultimate wisdom which, after so many necessary rebellions, is the rejection of all rebellion.

There are some who will say that this is nothing more than bourgeois morality. Unfortunately, however, we have had the opportunity to learn what happens to the world when moral technocracy replaces morality, just as the elegances of the précieuses left no time for making soup; the real bourgeois of today is the technocrat of back-room politics, the specialist in fragmentary efficiency. "The woman sterilized by the S.S. Blackshirts, the man put to bed with his naked sister, the mother clasping her child to her breast while they smashed its head in, the woman they invited to see her husband executed, those who escaped the gas chambers, all those who trembled day after day for years and are now nowhere at home": why were they persecuted—they and their brothers and sisters of all religions and all races—why are they still being persecuted, why will they still be persecuted tomorrow "in the midst of a great silence or the chatter of Pharisees"? It can only be because our world has been delivered up to an immense thoughtlessness, because this epoch of ours "tenses itself to build empires and attain the absolute," and wants "to transfigure the

Camus at his desk at Gallimard Publishers.

world before having exhausted it, to set it to rights before having understood it." Camus is no conservative, not out of principle, but because there is "nothing to conserve." But he is not so vain as to seek to remake the world without having found and gathered together all the values which justify its survival. He is able to see the forest for the trees, and he provides us with the reasons for doing what has to be done and the elementary though forgotten laws which make it possible to "mend what has been torn," to make "justice imaginable" and "happiness meaningful . . . Naturally, it is a superhuman task. But tasks are called superhuman when men take a long time to complete them, that is all."

He has taught us all again that "if the only solution is death, then we are not on the right road. The right road is the one which leads to life, to the sun." We must, with all the strength of our minds and hearts, say yes to the sun and to history, to the infinite world limited by the death of each of us.

And accept tragedy.

CHRONOLOGY

1913   November 7th: Albert, son of Lucien and Catherine Sintès Camus, born at Mondovi, department of Constantine, Algeria.

1914   The Great War. Lucien Camus, father of Albert Camus, killed in the First Battle of the Marne. His widow moves to the Belcourt quarter of Algiers.

1918   Albert Camus enrolled at the Belcourt primary school.

1923   May: his teacher Louis Germain puts Camus in for a scholarship examination. In October he enrolls at the Algiers lycée as a scholarship holder.

1930   Baccalauréat (final State examination after secondary education). Camus plays for Algiers University Racing Club football team. First attacks of sickness.

1931   Enrolled for higher university literature course. Meets Jean Grenier, professor and philosopher.

1933   Hitler in power. First marriage. Small administrative jobs to make a living.

1934   His divorce. Member of Algiers section of Communist Party. Campaigning for the Party among the Arabs.

1935   Resigns from Communist Party. On tour with Radio Algiers theatrical troupe. First pages of *Betwixt and Between*. Founds the Théâtre du Travail and takes part in the collective writing of a political play, *Revolt in Asturia*. More administrative jobs. Report for the Meteorological Institute on atmospheric pressures in the south of Algeria.

1936   The Popular Front in power in France. Léon Blum government. Franco revolution in Spain. Camus passes his examination for diploma of higher studies with a thesis on "The Relations between Hellenism and Christianity as Seen in the Works of Plotinus and St. Augustine." The Algiers publisher Charlot publishes *Revolt in Asturia*. Camus on tour through Algieria with Radio Algiers theatrical troupe. Camus palying juvenile leads in classical plays. Projected essay on Malraux.

1937   Disqualified for health reasons from taking part in examination (philosophy) for appointment to secondary and university teaching posts. The publisher Charlot in Algiers publishes *Betwixt and Between*. "The Team" founded, performances of *La Celestine, L'Article 330*, and other plays.

1938   A stay in Savoy and a trip to Florence. Camus refuses a teaching post in the lycée at Sidi-bel-Abbès. *Alger Républicain* founded. Pascal Pia takes Camus on as reporter. *Nuptials* published by Charlot. Camus writes *Caligula*. He stages *Brothers Karamazov* at "The Team."

1939   He begins writing *The Stranger* and finishes *The Minotaur or the Halt at Oran*. The *Kabylia Inquiry. Alger Républicain* changes to *Soir Républicain*. End of the Spanish Civil War.

Declaration of War. Journey to Greece put off. Camus volunteers for army service but is turned down for reasons of health. Trouble with Algiers censorship.

1940   Camus remarries. He is expelled from Algiers and goes to Paris where, on the recommendation of Pascal Pia, he is made editorial secretary with *Paris-Soir. The Stranger* is completed. German invasion of France. German troops enter Paris. Camus follows *Paris-Soir* when it moves to Clermont-Ferrand. Leaves the paper and settles for some months in Lyons.

September: Camus begins writing of *The Myth of Sisyphus*. Camus returns to Algeria and settles in Oran.

1941   February: *The Myth of Sisyphus* is completed.

1942   Return to France. In July, the Gallimard publishing house publishes *The Stranger*. Camus active in the Resistance in the Combat network. Allied landings in Algeria.

Camus is cut off from his family. *The Myth of Sisyphus* is published.

1943 A stay in the Massif Central mountains for reasons of health. Some time spent in Lyons and St. Etienne. The Combat Movement transfers Camus to Paris. The Gallimard publishing house engages him as publisher's reader. Clandestine publication of the newspaper *Combat.* Clandestine publication of the first *Letters to a German Friend.*

1944 May: *Cross Purpose* staged at the Théâtre des Mathurins. Last *Letter to a German Friend.*

Liberation of Paris. August 21st, the first issue of *Combat* to be freely distributed in the capital. Editorials by Camus.

1945 End of the war. Hiroshima.

Camus meets Gérard Philipe. *Caligula* staged at the Théâtre Hébertot. Numerous editorials in *Combat.*

1946 Camus visits the United States and addresses American students in New York.

1947 Camus leaves *Combat* as a result of a change in management and the newspaper's political views.

June: *The Plague* published. Camus receives the Critics' Prize.

1948 *State of Siege* staged at the Théâtre Marigny.

1949 Camus visits South America.

December: *The Just* staged at the Théâtre Hébertot.

1950 Camus working on *The Rebel.*

1951 October: *The Rebel* published. Prolonged polemics with the press of the extreme Left. As a result of a violent attack in the review *Les Temps Modernes,* Camus breaks with Sartre.

1952 November: Camus resigns from UNESCO after the admission of Franco Spain as a member. "*The Artist in Prison,*" preface to Oscar Wilde's *Ballad of Reading Gaol.*

1953 June: riots in East Berlin. Camus speaks out for the rioters. July: Camus returns to theatrical production. The Angers Festival, with *La Devotion à la Croix* and *Les Esprits.*

171

1954 Publication of *Summer*.
Beginnings of the war in Algeria.

1955 May: visit to Greece.
Articles in the newspaper *L'Express* on the Algerian problem. Performances of *Un Cas Interessant*, by Dino Buzzati, adapted by Camus, at the Théâtre La Bruyère.

1956 January: visit to Algeria. January 22nd: Appeal in favor of a civilian truce, at Algiers. May: *The Fall*. October: *Requiem for a Nun*, after William Faulkner, staged at the Théâtre des Mathurins. November: the Hungarian uprising. Camus calls on European writers to appeal to the United Nations.

1957 March: *Exile and the Kingdom*.
May: *Reflections on the Guillotine*, in collaboration with Arthur Koestler.
July: the Angers Festival, with *Caligula* and *Le Chevalier D'Olmedo*.
October 17th: the Stockholm Royal Academy awards the Nobel Prize for literature to Albert Camus "for his works throwing light on the problems facing the consciences of men."
December 10th: Albert Camus receives the Nobel Prize in Stockholm.

1958 A project for a political constitution for Algeria. Publication of *Algerian Reports (Actuelles III)*.

1959 February: *The Possessed* staged at the Théâtre Antoine. Camus begins work on a novel, *The First Man*.
October: the touring company leaves for the provinces with *The Possessed*.

1960 January 4th: death of Albert Camus.

BIBLIOGRAPHY

1. Works

Caligula and Three Other Plays [*Misunderstanding; State of Siege; Just Assassins*]. New York, 1962.
Exile and the Kingdom. New York, 1958.
The Fall. New York, 1957.
Lyrical and Critical Essays. New York, 1968.
The Myth of Sisyphus and Other Essays. New York, 1955.
Notebooks, Vol. 1: 1935–1942; Vol. 2: 1942–1951. New York, 1963; 1965.
The Plague. New York, 1948.
The Possessed. New York, 1960.
The Rebel: An Essay on Man in Revolt. New York, 1954.
Resistance, Rebellion and Death. New York, 1961.
The Stranger. New York, 1946.

2. Biography and Criticism

BREE, GERMAINE. *Albert Camus.* New York, 1964
————, ed. *Camus: A collection of Critical Essays.* Englewood Cliffs, N.J., 1961.
CHAMPIGNY, ROBERT. *Pagan Hero: An Interpretation of Meursault in Camus' Stranger.* Translated by Rowe Portis. Philadelphia, 1969.
CRUICKSHANK, JOHN. *Albert Camus and the Literature of Revolt.* New York, 1959.
FALK, EUGENE. *Types of Thematic Structure.* Chicago, 1967.

HANNA, THOMAS. *Lyrical Existentialists*. New York, 1962.

—————. *The Thought and Art of Albert Camus*. Chicago, 1959.

KING, ADELE. *Albert Camus*. New York, 1965.

MAQUET, ALBERT. *Albert Camus, the Invincible Summer*. New York, 1958.

MERTON , THOMAS, *Commentary on The Plaque*. New York, n.d.

ONIMUS, JEAN. *Albert Camus and Christianity*. University, Ala., 1969.

PARKER, EMMETT. *Albert Camus: The Artist in the Arena*. Madison, Wis., 1965.

PETERSEN, CAROL. *Albert Camus*. Translated by Alexander Gode. New York, 1968.

POLLMANN, LEO. *Sartre and Camus: The Literature of Existence*. Translated by Helen Sebba. New York, 1971.

RHEIN, PHILLIP. *Albert Camus*. New York, n.d.

—————. *The Urge to Live: A Comparative Study of Franz Kafka's Der Prozess and Albert Camus' L'Etranger*. New York, 1964.

ROEMING, ROBERT. *Camus Bibliography*. Madison, Wis., 1968.

SCOTT, NATHAN. *Camus*. New York, n.d.

THODY, PHILIP. *Albert Camus: A Study of His Work*. New York, 1959.

WILLHOITE, FRED. *Beyond Nihilism: Albert Camus' Contribution to Political Thought*. Baton Rouge, La., 1968.